In The Lands of Buddha

Travels of a pre-teen in Asia

By Joshua Navez-Barry

Photography by Ren Navez

Additional photography by Shawn Barry and Joshua Navez-Barry

A Flaming Serpent Publication

Book Design by Ren Navez
Maps based on United Nations Maps

ISBN # 1-4404-0665-0

Flaming Serpent Publishing
POB 2487
Venice, CA 90294

COVER PHOTOS:
FRONT: Josh at Ta Prohm Temple in Angkor Wat, Cambodia
BACK: Josh at a Pagoda in Yangon, Myanmar

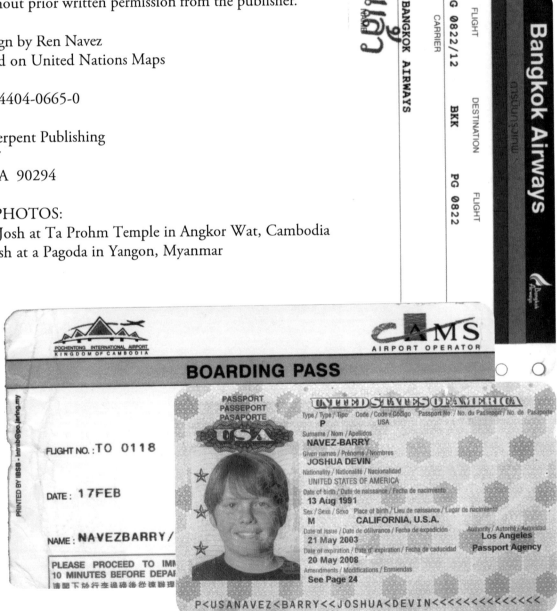

Joshie
Is
Hungry

above the orchid
below the ferns

Preface

A couple of years ago, Shawn and I realized a long held plan of taking our 12-year old son Joshua to live in Southeast Asia for a year. Both of us had spent a great deal of time traveling earlier in life, and we wanted to impart our love for the diversity of the cultures of the world to our son. We were fortunate to have other family members and friends join us for parts of the journey. Josh skipped 7th grade while we supposedly "home-schooled" him on the road, but in fact his education for the year was his experience of this part of the world.

This book is a compilation of some of his observations and tales written at the time, along with photos from the trip.

Ren Navez

Christmas in the town of Pai, Thailand

Acknowledgements

There are many people I would like to thank for making this trip so special and life changing. The first two people I need to thank are the architects of the trip, my mom and dad - Shawn and Ren. It was their ideas, money and love that made this trip possible. The next person is I want to thank is Terry, a great friend and our guide for the first couple of months in Thailand - he taught me things about coexisting with different cultures that continue to influence me today. I would like to thank Colleen and Mike, my grandmother and uncle, for adding immeasurable amounts of laughter and gaiety to our adventures; to Tiger and Alex for deciding to join in on part of the trip with us and for their wacky antics that are so much fun; to Eamon, Cole and Jolie who came for the last few weeks of the trip and giving the voyage one last boom before heading home; to Bui, a man on Koh Phi-Phi who taught me how to firedance; to all the dive crews I've had from Koh Tao, Koh Chang, Koh Phi-Phi, and the island of Lembongan near Bali; to Sam for bringing us into her home full of love and for being one wild and fun individual; to Richmond for taking us diving; to Lynda and Dave for bringing me canned refried beans (growing up in southern California Latin food is a required part of my diet, and as there is almost no Latin food in Southeast Asia, I missed it terribly) and for being such happy positive people through the worst of times; to Debbie for being a better monkey than the ones at the show; to Patsy for embracing her true jungle-woman self; to TC for volunteering me for my first chug-a-lug contest; and to Sam from the Mulberry farm for teaching me so much about culture and providing me with memories I'll never forget. There are two people who I would especially like to thank for all the happiness and love we shared, Delphine and Zorro, two exceptionally nice travelers who, like us, were taking time to travel southeast Asia. They contributed to my character change and world perceptions more than they will ever realize, and I hope and pray that maybe someday we'll meet again. I want to thank all of the people we met along the way, and everyone who made this trip as magic as possible.

Shawn & Ren in Koh Lanta

Mike & Nanny in Koh Phi Phi

Terry working on his yoga

Josh, Lynda & David on a ferry boat

Debbie and her monkey

Josh, Ren, Tiger, Alex, Zorro, Delphine

Patsy & TC came for the beach

Josh, Cole, Alex & Eamon in Bali

Table of Contents

Prologue - 9
Spiders And Shots - 10

<u>Thailand</u>

Thailand Information - 14
Food, Glorious Food - 18
Bathroom Adventures - 20
Elephant Trekking - 22
Theravada Buddhism - 24
Wats, Stupas & Statues - 26
A Joy Ride - 29
Cobra Show - 27
Bargaining - 30
Damned Roosters - 31
Scuba Diving - 32
Venturing Through The Deep - 33
Sell me a Beer - 36
The Girl Next Door - 37
Lynda's Bad Day - 40
Reggae Pub - 41

<u>Cambodia</u>

Cambodia Information - 44
Zorro - 47
Bayon Boys - 53
Landmine Experiences - 54
Bokor - 55

<u>Laos</u>

Laos Information - 62
Pi Mai Lao - 63
Pak Ou Caves - 65
Mulberry Farm - 66
Tat Kuang Si Waterfall - 68

<u>Myanmar</u>

Myanmar Information - 74
Inle Lake - 76
Hell Ride to Bagan - 78
Bike Riding in Bagan - 80
Best Restaurant in Yangon - 84

Transport - 90
Reflections - 92
Epilogue - 92

<u>Appendices</u>

Joshie's Hungry! - 94
Hill Tribes - 95
Hotels - 96
Thai Glossary - 98

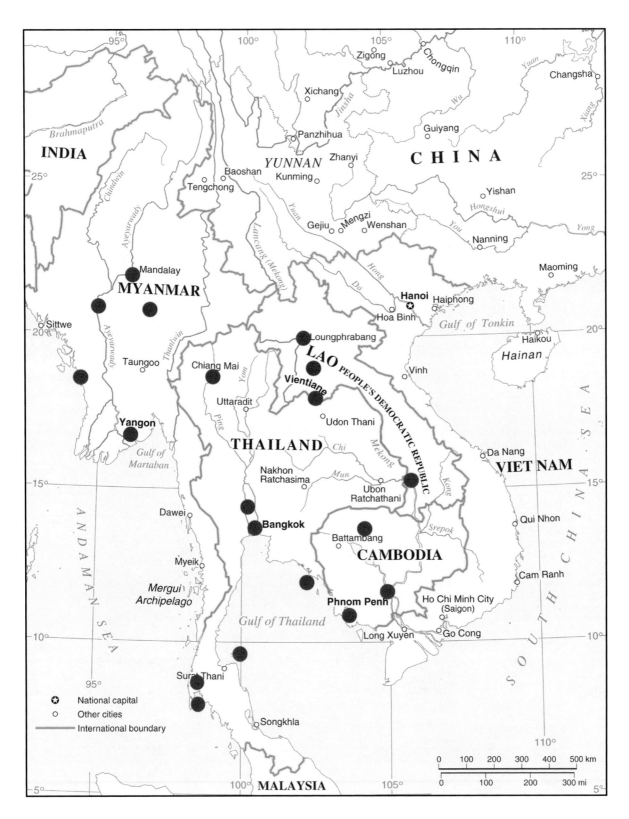

Areas we visited shown in red

Prologue

The first time I heard about it, I was in the first grade. For that matter, I don't actually remember it, but I recall a small part. I have a very strange memory. I can barely remember two years ago when I graduated from the fifth grade, but I can remember how many times I choked on chives in my soup five days ago (Please note: I hate chives!). If I don't forget something from a while ago, I forget something from two minutes earlier. See? There it goes again. I forgot to tell you what I'm talking about!

As I said before, the first time I heard about it was in first grade. The thought of going to India, Indonesia, New Zealand, Australia, Thailand and other countries for a year seemed too overwhelming and amazing. Maybe that's why I can't remember it. Anyway, by third grade, I could not forget it, not that it was on my mind constantly, but it was always in that dark corner, laughing at me when I thought of it. Slowly it grew, and with it so did curiosity, and finally ideas. By the fourth grade, questions arose. Questions that varied from "What do we eat?" to "What are the languages?" and finally to "No, I don't like the sound of that hotel, how about the…?" But as all things in life must be balanced, with happiness and joy, there must be sorrow and misery. When the anticipation was at it's highest, my family had decided that Australia and New Zealand would cost too much. From threats of wars with Pakistan and not enough time, India was crossed out from the list. We couldn't just go to Thailand and Indonesia, so we decided to go to Laos, Cambodia, Myanmar or Vietnam. In reality, we knew it wouldn't be decided until we were there.

Before the fifth grade, this subject was mentioned only with my parents, but when I was 10, my cousins and I started to discuss it. They knew about our plans, we just never talked about it. One day when we were watching that "Survivor" show, and they were on islands, we were talking about how we could forage for food, build houses, make animal traps, and so on. When we watched the movies "Robinson Crusoe" and "Swiss Family Robinson" our ideas and imagination expanded farther. We talked it over with our parents, and they said, "Where could this be done?" We thought "of course, our trip!" And that was when I learned that my cousins would visit for a while, like for 2 months out of our year!

A while before we departed, all my school friends, close friends, and family knew of our trip. In my yearbook, friends wrote things like "see you in a year" or "miss you while you're away." Suddenly, like thunder, a new idea struck me. I realized that, when I was away for a while, I would be sad. Like a pin at my heart, I realized that I wouldn't hear about Hailey's threats, Coleman's endless jokes, Al's annoying acts, Eamon's crazy ideas, Libby's evilness, and so much more. The day I woke up to leave on this amazing journey, a thought crossed my mind:

"I had waited years for this day to happen, and on the day I was to leave on this exotic adventure, in the blink of an eye I realized that I wished it was any day, but today."

Spiders and Shots

There are things in the world that I do not enjoy. There are some things that I dislike. But, there are only two things that I hate. One is spiders. Now don't get me wrong, I do think they are fascinating, the way some can jump, some can walk on water, and weave such amazing webs. But there is something about the way they crawl, how quick they are and their odd traits and habits. As you see, I have mild arachnophobia.

The other thing I hate - shots. The truth is that the suspense kills me. Waiting for a needle to be jabbed into my arm is much worse than the pain. Actually, I have a funny story behind shots.

The first time I can remember, I must have been around 4 or 5 years old, I was waiting for a shot, as I was about to get injected my mom

4 inch spider in Au Luk Cave, Thailand

said, "Look away Josh, look away." I looked away and suddenly the nurse decided she didn't do something right, so she took the syringe away and went to go get another. Meanwhile another shot, the shot of suspense was impaling my brain with it's painful waiting. Ever since that day, I haven't been able to look away.

Unfortunately, I have to get shots so I don't get Japanese encephalitis, polio or other diseases. There are a ton of spiders in Southeast Asia. Guess I'm going to have to do what every species has learned to do - Adapt!

Josh in the Sierra Nevavda mountains shortly before leaving the country

For me a foreigner (farang) from america,
an elephant trek sounded like something out of a dream. To be able to
go along a trail for weeks, on an
elephants back, foraging food, sleeping
in the jungle getting to play with
monkeys, seeing a secret waterfall,
excetera........, this is, of course, what
every kid dreams of when the think
about a jungle expedition, adventure, or
such. This is what T.V. illustrates,
and it is incorrect as I found
out. When I had learned that
the elephant ride only lasted
about an hour, I was crushed.
Of course we had already signed
up, so it was too late. As we
were arriving, I confirmed to myself
that it was just practice, so when
we went overnight sometime in
the future, we would be ready.
As the trek started, I was
asked if I wanted to ride on the neck,
or in the seat with my uncle and
mom. Taking it as an adventure, I mounted
on to the neck. Soon we were off
on the trek and yet again, hopes

Reclining Buddha, Wat Po, Bangkok

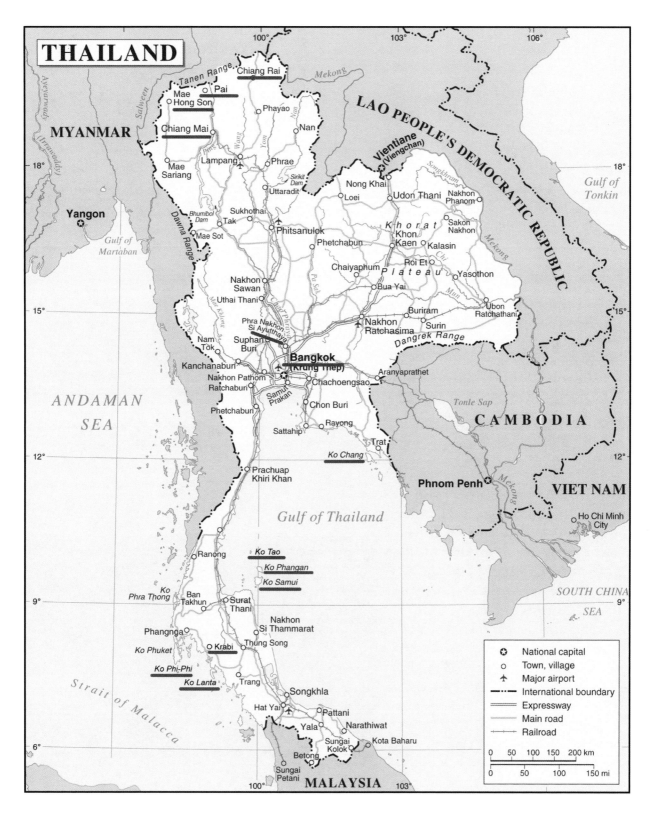

Places we visited underlined in red

Thailand Information

Area: 517,000 square kilometers
       (slightly smaller than Texas)
Capital: Bangkok
Main Language: Thai
Money: US$1 = About 36 Baht
Population: 62 million
Religion: 95% of the country is
       Theravada Buddhist

Government / Politics

Thailand is a democracy, however they have a king, his majesty Bhumibol Adulydej, who the Thai people love and admire. Thailand means "land of the free" it was never colonized as were most of its neighboring countries; but they were occupied by the Japanese during World War II.

Holidays

The two largest Thai holidays are Loy Kratong and Songkran. Loy Kratong is in November; it is celebrated on the full moon night of the 12th lunar month everywhere in Thailand. This holiday is to give thanks to the goddess of the river, as it was celebrated in India hundreds of years ago. Loy Kratong is celebrated by making small vessels out of banana tree trunks and banana leaves. They then add flowers, candles, coins and either a few strands of hair or fingernails to be put on the Kratong (banana vessel). Once made, the candle is lit and they are pushed out to sea or into a river. A wish is made as the Kratong floats away to the river goddess. It is one of the most beautiful things I saw during the entire

Head from a Buddha statue overgrown by a tree at Ayutthia Temples

Making "Loy Kratons" to float on the ocean

Songkran revelers in Bangkok

Taking classes in Thailand has been made very easy for the foreigner, they are offered almost anywhere in the country. They include: Thai and Asian cooking, where they take you to the farm to see the vegetables grow, then the market to learn to shop for yourself and only after these two steps do you get in the kitchen and begin to cook; Thai massage, with a variety of styles and length of classes; Muay Thai basic training, and more advanced training if you're there for a while; Buddhist/meditation classes, taught by monks in the temples; many languages including Thai and local hill tribe dialects; and many other classes most wouldn't expect to find!

trip, a sea of candles and flowers floating away on the vast ocean.

Songkran is in April to celebrate the Thai New Year. To celebrate this, every city becomes a giant water war. Everyone in the city participates in a citywide water fight! There is no mercy, whether you're in a car, or whether you tell them not to, no mercy, none, ever.

Sport

Muay Thai is the national passion of Thailand. In this form of boxing, before the match, both fighters bow to all four corners while a band plays Thai ceremonial music, once this ritual is done, which usually lasts about 3-4 minutes, the two fighters attack each other. There are a maximum of five rounds in a match, there are judges who give a point to a fighter if no one is knocked out in the round, and the first fighter to get three points wins. The fighters are allowed to use just about any part of their body, and trust me, more times than not, you would rather take a punch than one of the kicks these warriors can dish out!

Learning Thai massage techniques

15

Two places in the North worth visiting

Chaing Mai is an old city in the north of Thailand that shows the modern-day culture of Thailand exquisitely. Chaing Mai is a city enclosed by ancient walls, with temples throughout the city. It has some of the country's best markets for shopping, including the Sunday Market, and the legendary Chaing Mai night bazaar which has the best food imaginable. The best way to travel around Chaing Mai is by renting a bike to work your way down the back alleys to all of the most popular locations.

Pai is a four-hour drive north from Chaing Mai. It is a small friendly valley town, right on a river, surrounded by rice paddies, caves and hot springs-probably my favorite town in all of Thailand. It is the best. A great place to stay is the Golden Hut Bungalows, which is close to the town, and your view from the balcony is of miles of rice paddies and a river.

A few memorable activities that you can participate in here are river rafting, elephant riding, caving, buying arsenals of fireworks and blowing them off, and so much more!

Buddhist Monks visiting the ancient temples of Sukkothai in central Thailand

Festival in Bo Sang, a town near Chiang Mai reknowned for their paper umbrellas and fans

A quick review of some Thai islands
("Koh" means island)

Koh Phi Phi has its main village built on an isthmus between two hilly islands, there are no cars on this island, and the fastest mode of transportation is biking. It is one of the most beautiful places I have ever been to in my life. The palm trees go right up to the clear turquoise water, and the white sand reflects in your soul, it is incredible. The scuba diving that Koh Phi Phi offers is some of the best in Thailand. For anyone who has seen the movie or read the book <u>The Beach</u>, it was filmed on a neighboring island. When the tsunami hit Thailand, it wiped through Koh Phi-Phi, maiming it, but I'm sure the Island has recovered.

Koh Chang is a remote Island with an excellent blend of culture and paradise. Diving is really good if the sea isn't murky. If the day and water is clear, you'll have an incredible diving experience. The palms line the chrystalline white sand beaches, it is truly a great island.

Koh Samui is a major tourist island. It is overcrowded and highly westernized; this island is mainly for the tourist and the less adventurous type but it is still great and a lot of fun. Koh

Fishing boat off Koh Tao

Samui is one of the only islands that have an airport.

Koh Phangan is small island next to Samui that I only saw part of so I can't judge it all, but wherever I went, I loved! Mae Had is a beautiful secluded area with just 15 small bungalows on the entire beach. It is good for snorkeling, and the village is just 5 houses turned into stores and restaurants. It's one of the most laid-back places we went on the entire trip.

If you don't dive, there is no point in going to Koh Tao, this island is all about diving. But if you are a diver, it is one of the best places in Thailand. Every hotel here can supply diving instructors and boats.

*"Longtail" boats
on Koh Phi Phi*

17

Food, Glorious Food!

Our favorite restaurant in Chiang Mai

One of the biggest cultural differences to experience in Asia is a complete diet swap. The burgers, burritos, and pizza of home transforms into curry, pad thai and som tam (green papaya salad). The new range of delicacies available is overwhelming. The multitude of curries - red, green, yellow, masaman, kao soy, and others with unpronounceable names, are now main dishes we often eat, as they are cheap and delicious. Asian cultures have various styles of noodles, many with only small tweaks of change from each other, but they make an entirely different taste. Perhaps the most exciting part of trying the new foods are the fruits. The bounty of nature fruit-wise in Asia is unending; there are lychees, star fruits, papaya, mango, Mangosteen, custard apple, rambutan, dragon fruit, longans, jackfruit and more. The best part is that all of those, plus more, can get turned into juices (fresh fruit, washed, cut and blended right in front of you) at the abundant juice shops. Not thirsty? Right in front is a small Pad See Ew (noodles) cart that often sell food of better taste than inside many restaurants. Just had noodles? Twenty feet away is a satay (grilled meat on a bamboo skewer) stand that also happens to have the infamous toasted coconut milk that really does put all of those crappy brown coconuts at Albertsons to shame. There's really only one thing to say: the food is exceptional.

Amazing new fruits!

Local fairs have wide varieties of food

Market bounty with the new and unknown

Tofu making in Burma

Dried squid on a stick, an acquired taste

Fried crickets are easier than the cockroaches

Enjoying finger foods and "live shrimp" on a lakeside picnic

Toasted coconut milk is the best!

Bathroom Adventures

In Thailand, I learned there were many things I had to be prepared for, and for every problem there was a solution. As examples: for bugs there is a mosquito net, or for a cold, there's medicine. One thing, however, I didn't expect, was a problem in the bathroom. But on the fifth day in Bangkok, I walked into the restroom in a nice, small Thai restaurant. I closed the door, turned around, and saw a pleasant little room, with a clean toilet. I had to take a dump very badly. After 7 minutes of "doing that thing", I looked for some toilet paper. I couldn't see any, so I turned in the other direction. Still nothing. I started panicking because all that was in the room was soap, a bucket of water, and what looked like a showerhead. Once I calmed down, I decided that I would wipe my butt with my boxers, and then throw them away. I could do that or walk around with crap in my pants! I decided not to go with the latter, so 4 minutes later, I was boxer-less! Of course afterward I learned that I was supposed to wash my butt with the shower head thing.

"We call it a 'spritzer,'" Terry said. I looked at him, dumb stricken. Terry laughed. Terry, in a matter of fact voice, said, "It's a lot better than toilet paper once you get used to it." Still perplexed I said, "So I'm supposed to stick this 'spritzer' under my butt, push a button, and wash it out?"

"Pretty much," he replied and laughed again.

What an "interesting" experience that was! I'll "correct" myself next time.

Khao San Road, the center for backpacking travelers in Bangkok, and often their first stop in Asia

A typical streetside restaurant, Pok Pok was a favorite place in Chiang Mai

It took me a while to consider it; it took me ever longer to do it. I could pee, no problem, but to take a crap in a hole in the ground where you squat, was out of my league. Or was it? When you got to go, you got to go!

Debbie and I were shopping for pants because I had forgotten to put any on. Yes, I had clothes on! Normally, I wear shorts. The only reason we were getting them is because you are advised to wear long pants when you go elephant riding, which is what we were doing later that day. Midway down the beach, I started to get stomach cramps. When we got to a place that sells pants, I forced a smile and said "Hongnam utinae kap (where is the bathroom)?" The vendor led me along a small path to a tin shack with two rooms. In one of the rooms, the one with the open door, there was a man washing clothes. Someone was inside the other room, which was the bathroom. Waiting for the man to finish "going for the gold," I was being bitten by red ants. When he was done, I carefully stepped in and squatted down and "ppffuffpp" out it went! So relieved to be finished, I looked for something to wipe my butt with, and there was nada. Nothing. Zip. Zero. Uh-oh. Not wearing boxers this time, but only my swim trunks. I wiped my butt with my hand, and held it under a jet of water with soap for five minutes… I've got to get this bathroom thing figured out! I have to do what the locals do, it's their country and I'm the guest!

Elephant Trekking

For a farang (foreigner) from America, an elephant trek sounded like something out of dream. To be able to go along a trail for weeks on an elephant's back, foraging for food, sleeping in the jungle, getting to play with monkeys, seeing a secret waterfall, etc... this is what every kid dreams of when thoughts turn to a jungle adventure. This is what TV illustrates, and it is incorrect as I found out.

When I heard that the elephant ride would only last about an hour, I was crushed. Of course we had already signed up, so it was too late to leave. As we were arriving I assured myself that it was just practice, so when we went overnight sometime in the future, we would be ready. As the trek started, I was asked if I wanted to ride on the neck or in the seat with my uncle and mom. Taking it as an adventure, I mounted the neck. Soon we were off on the trek and yet again, hopes were destroyed. There was a man holding a rope attached to the elephant, walking it, just like you would walk a dog. The reason that this bothered me was that I wanted to control the elephant, not let someone else do it for me. So as we went down the path, it was nice and I had to admit, I was enjoying myself. Then

Initial suspiscions....

become a lifelong love and respect

as we started to go up rocks the elephant moved his head around and me, being on the neck, I went vertical. Luckily, my mom and uncle grabbed my arms and pulled me upright, but now since they've grabbed my arms, I had no balance, so I was sliding everywhere. They nearly let go of me a few times, they were laughing so hard! Once we found a break in the rocks, they pulled me up into the chair. I cannot even explain in words how hard we were laughing at this experience, I don't know if I've ever laughed so hard before in my life! My mom was in tears, and I was nearly there. When the trek was over, she asked my opinion of the elephant ride.

"Too short," I said.

"Well," she replied. "The rides in Chiang Mai will be longer, maybe an overnight."

Suddenly, dreams were reborn.

Theraveda Buddhism

One of the most important parts of the culture of Southeast Asia is the religion. The way that this is shown is through the Wats. A Wat is a Buddhist temple; they are usually built out of cement or teak, and often have sloped roofs with carvings of the Naga dragon on the four corners. Inside there is an altar to pray at. The altar usually has at least one Buddha image, an incense bowl, and some candles burning. The Khmer, Thai, Laos and Myanmar Buddha's are different from the Chinese Buddha. The Chinese Buddha is the obese Buddha, usually laughing, sometimes carrying a bundle over his back. However, the Southeast Asian Buddha is slim, has long ears, hair, and is usually found in either a sitting, standing, or reclining position. As in many religions, there are monks, who live at the temples in the monastery. Monks aren't the super kung-fu karate masters as they are too often shown on TV. They simply live at the monastery and pray to Buddha. Of course there are other things, like ceremonies and restrictions, but that's the basic monk's life. It seems like there are a couple million temples throughout Southeast Asia. The smallest towns always have at least one or two temples. Trust me, on a hot day, walking into a temple and sitting down, is so quiet, so peaceful, it's great!

Monks chanting in Wat Cheddi Luang, Chiang Mai

Ancient Sukothai Temple Complex, central Thailand

I would like to relate the story of the Buddha. Once there was a great kingdom in present day Nepal. When the queen gave birth to her first son, a priest predicted that her son would be either a great acetic or a powerful king. The current king, wanting his son only to become a powerful ruler, did not allow him to see old age, sickness, death, sadness, or religious articles so as to prevent him from becoming a monk who would help people and renounce all of his possessions. So, Siddhartha, the king's son, the next Buddha, never knew about any of these things his father took away. But one day, wanting to know more of the world, Prince Siddhartha ran away, and when he went into the real world he saw two old people weeping over the death of their son, which filled him with sorrow. But then he saw a monk who, although all this sadness was around, seemed perfectly content while meditating. This inspired him so much that he renounced everything he owned, including his wife and child, and went to meditate. He sat under a Bodhi tree for three days, starving himself, so when an old woman asked him if he wanted any rice, he took some and gobbled it down. He was so ashamed of himself that he pledged to meditate under a Bodhi tree without moving or eating until he obtained enlightenment. On the seventh day, he became enlightened and traveled, teaching others what he knew. In Southeast Asia they base their calendar year starting with the year Buddha became enlightened. For them it's 2549 , not 2006!

Wats, Stupas & Statues

A 'wat' is the name for a Buddhist monastery in Thailand, Cambodia and Laos. Because of the prevalence of Buddhism, even the rural villages have wats. Since they are a sacred place to honor and learn the teachings of Buddha, the campus and buildings are made splendid, with multiple pillars, intricate carvings and paintings covering whole buildings and ceilings, lots of gold or gold-leaf plus bright colors everywhere. The heads of dragons are carved into almost every rooftop corner of buildings, and much more, varying from Wat to Wat. But the magnificence of wats is in the peace that exists within their walls. For example, Wat Chana Songhkram is on Khan San Road, one of the most crowded streets in the huge city of Bangkok. The street is loud and dusty, but if you take one single step into the grounds of the wat, then the sound of people shouting and cars, the smell of burned chili's from roadside carts, and the calamity of being rushed and busy all vanish instantly with the soft sound of monks chanting and the sweet smelling serenity of temporary nirvana.

Southeast Asia is littered with 'stupas', mounded forms of clay with a spire that originally were made to hold relics of the Buddha. Some still do but most just have an image of the Buddha and are a symbolic object of veneration. Every Wat has at least one stupa. Traditionally, a stupa is made up of five parts: a square base, a hemispherical dome, a conical spire, a crescent moon and a circular disc. Each of the five parts is rich in metaphor, primarily to illustrate teachings of the Buddha.

Statues and other images of the Buddha are also found everywhere, especially around wats. Every image of Buddha must be revered and treated with respect. Most of them depict the Buddha in a seated meditation, but he can also be shown in other postures such as standing, walking or reclining. His hands always express one of the six major gestures called "mudras", each having a different meaning.

Evening chants at Doi Suthep in Chiang Mai

Painted cieling of a small Wat in Chiang Rai

A row of Buddhas at the ancient temple of
Ayuthia are given cermonial sarongs

Stupa at Wat
Bupparam in
Chiang Mai

Ket Karam Stupa in Chiang Mai

The grounds of Wat Po in Bangkok

Monks are always eager to talk

A Joy Ride

Just imagine Asian elephants. Most people will never get to see one, or they'll see it in a zoo. However, I got the better end of the deal. I got to ride 6 times. This is the story of, probably my first or second favorite ride. It all started in Pai...

We pulled up at the place pretty early in the morning. And as soon as my mom, dad and I could, we were on the elephant known as Joy. We cruised through a teak forest, seeing incredibly beautiful sights in the early morning. After about an hour we headed back, without a care in the world. Once back, we changed into swimsuits and mounted onto the elephant bareback, and headed for the river. At the river my mom and dad hopped off to take pictures. The "mahout" (the elephant's commander and trainer) and I rode the elephant into the river, where we played a game: the elephant tries to throw me off his neck, and I try to stay on. The mahout meanwhile rode the elephant like a surfboard. In the end, the elephant easily won.

The elephant and the mahout are together for life. Our mahout was sick once and had to leave to go to a hospital and his elephant, "Joy" stopped eating and moped until he returned. To take the job of a mahout is a great responsibility, the mahout must accept the challenge of coexisting with the elephant for the rest of their lives. It is a very serious job, but a rewarding one if accepted.

Family road trip in Pai

Swimming with Joy

28

Cobra Show

Snake trainer playing with cobras

<T>he cobra show was amazing. "Cheating death" - that's what the man giving the cobra show was doing. He was poking venomous cobras in the nose with his finger. Later I found out most cobras can't see at certain angles, so they are easily blindsided! He played with some water snakes that can strike so fast a person won't know what's coming. He caught two water snakes with his hands, and the third in his mouth! He got onto his hands and knees and slowly bent over the snake and caught the snake's throat in his mouth. Then he brought out a python and put it into the small pool in the arena where he was battling the snakes. The pool was about 8 feet wide and 6 feet deep, and the handler jumped in after the python. Even though anyone could tell that the "battle" was fake, it was still cool to watch the man wrestle with the snake. Throughout the show there was a group of people who kept getting freaked out when the snake handler would try to move toward them with the snakes. It was humorous, watching them run away. Then the handler asked me if I wanted to put a cobra on my neck and kiss it, and I said, "YES."

My mom said "They would never allow this in the states!"

Soon there were about 11 wide-eyed people looking at me. The announcer stated: "See, he's brave."

One person said: "Not brave, crazy." Everyone laughed. I loved it!

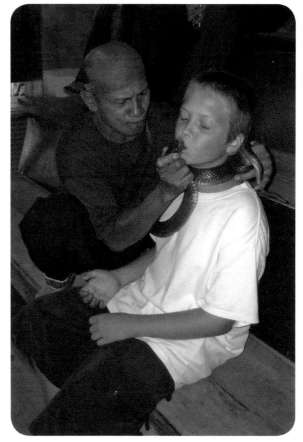

I get to kiss a cobra!

Bargaining

In Santa Monica, I would walk into a store, look around, find something I like, and I buy it. Here it is so different. For starters, you walk into a store, find something, ask how much it costs, bargain, and buy it. People have to bargain for everything even food or lodging. It's rather funny, because even if the seller starts off at an unreasonable price; it's still cheaper than back home. For example: when I was buying a sarong:

"Gib baht (how much)?" I said.

"Song roi ha sib (three hundred and fifty)," he replies.

"Dai mai, dai mai, lot noy dai mai (no, no, no, lower the price)."

"Tow rai (how much)?"

"Song rai (two hundred)."

"Mai, mai, sam rai (no, no, no, three hundred)."

I shake my head and start to walk away.

"Kap, kap, song rai, song rai (yes, yes, 200, 200)."

I bought the sarong for two hundred baht, which is about 5 US dollars. It's sort of funny though, because 350 baht is about $8.75, and I've seen sellers in the states sell them for double that price and not as nice. My Mom and Dad let me do most of the bargaining as I know the language the best and love the challenge.

Admiring swords in the Chiang Mai night market

Central Market of Pai

Shopping in Som Pet Market, Chiang Mai

Often, bargains would come to you

Damned Roosters

Cock-a-doodle-doo, cock-a-doodle-doo," the roosters called at 3 a.m. in the town of Pai. "Cock-a-doodle-doo, cock-a-doodle-doo," the bloody roosters screamed. I've been awake for 3 hours, listening to those noisy roosters. "Cock-a-doodle-doo, cock-a-doodle-doo." There they were again. In Pai, at around midnight, the weather gets freezing. "Cock-a-doodle-doo, cock-a-doodle-doo." I woke up because I was cold. Couldn't get back to sleep because of those twisted roosters.

"Cock-a-doodle-doo, cock-a-doodle-doo." I swear I'm going to kill them.

"Cock-a-doodle-doo, cock-a-doodle-doo," wailed those annoying, condemned, damnable roosters.

"Cock-a-doodle-doo, cock-a-doodle-doo."

Aaaahh! Euggh!

Silence.

"What!" I thought.

Silence.

A cricket chirped.

Silence.

A frog burped.

Silence.

"Eerg, raah, rough, eerg, raah, fough, eerg, raah, rough." The dogs barked. Their yelling must have gone on for an hour.

"Eerg, raah, rough, eerg, raah, fough, eerg, raah, rough."

And my parents wondered why I was tired in the morning?

The culprit disturbing a "Spirit House"

Finally, some rest!

31

Scuba Diving

Final check before dropping in

Before entering the water, the equipment is heavy and awkward. Then you jump in - and it's a rush. You take in your first breath; it feels like being born again. After pushing down on the "inflate" button, once again, you're above the water. Out goes the regulator. With the jacket (BC) that makes you float inflated, your adrenaline decreases a bit. In about 7 seconds, you're begging the instructor to allow you to submerge......

By your 100th breath, the 15th time you've equalized, and the 8th time you're given the "OK" sign, you've gotten the simple parts down. By the end of the 10th dive, you've gotten the hang of it. It truly is a wild experience and quite amazing to swim with sharks, observe fish, and do so many things that you couldn't do on land. I am extremely careful underwater. I am always observant to be sure that I don't hurt or touch anything unless I am 100% certain it is okay for the environment. Such as a sea cucumber, you can pick them up, or a strand of kelp, if they are accidentally touched it'll be okay.

I've waited so long to scuba dive. Ever since I snorkeled off Catalina Island, I've wondered what it would be like to dive. It is amazing, absolutely amazing. I can barely describe how wonderful,

fun, exciting, and sometimes scary it is. When you're neutrally buoyant (weightless and floating), it feels as if I'm flying. It truly does. Almost weightless underwater, I can do things that I couldn't do on land such as flying summersaults, cartwheels and back flips. Anyone who's a fan of the Matrix (like me!) could finally be their own Neo. My friend Cole, who owns all of the Matrix movies, could spend hours, realizing what it would be like to be Keanu Reeves.

Dive boat at Koh Phi-Phi Ley

Venturing Through the Deep

ASTONISHING. That's probably the best word for diving. I learned in Koh Phi Phi (Pee-Pee) the first level, and in Koh Chang, I completed the advanced course. I love these beautiful islands. Koh Phi-Phi and Koh Chang each have their own type of great marine life and corals with the thousands of varied aquatic organisms. In Phi-Phi, I dove with a dive shop called Island Divers, in Koh Chang with Water World Diving and in Koh Tao with Coral Grand Divers, all three places had excellent and nice dive instructors, the only difference would be the quality of the equipment.

Diving is breathtaking; it makes me think twice about life, about others, about lots of things. For me, it's as much an emotional experience as it is a physical experience. Both are fantastic. Life on a reef is so simple, yet so complex at the same time. One day, a predator might eat you, or an anchor might crush your house, or you may have to search for a mate, so even though the task is simple, it is complex to complete it. To escape a predator is easy for the fish , stay in a group and avoid feeding areas. But what if a current sweeps you away, or a shark singles you out, or what if you get caught in a net? It's also incredible to know that you and your buddy have put your lives in each other's hands. You don't want to be 35 meters (about 116 feet) deep, and suddenly have your buddy hate you. If one of you runs out of air, you need the other. It truly does make you think.

I want to tell some of my experiences while diving. Once, near the end of the dive in Chumphon, a dive site near Koh Tao, we were near the buoy line that we ascended on when the most miraculous thing happened. Before I can tell you what happened, you have to understand the surroundings.

Pointing out feather worms

Getting dive site instructions

Bliss in a school of baraccudas

My dad, our dive instructor, two other people and I were at the edge of a pinnacle, to our right is the pinnacle top (15 meters submerged, or about 50 feet), and to our left is a drop to about 24 meters, which then continues to go down to 40 meters and deeper. This area is sandy with few fish. The pinnacle itself is rock with tropical corals, anemones, lot of fish, sea cucumbers, shells, etc. We were slightly above the pinnacle, when suddenly; I look out into this deep-sea void and wow! I saw a 2 meter long black-tip reef shark! Reef sharks are rare, but Chumphon is the place to see them. I quickly point the sight out to my dad and our dive master Lee, when I see that there are now two sharks! We descended to 18 meters watching the two, but wait! Now there are three sharks! The sharks are at 30 or 50 meters, so we stay above due to good visibility. We watched them for 5 minutes, fading in and out of the deep, when they come back with 5! Five black-tip reef sharks! Three of them are two meters, one a meter and a half, and the fifth, two and a half meters! We watched them for another 5 minutes, when our dive master unfortunately says, "We have to go," but just as we turn to leave, I see a sixth one coming out of the blue!

While we were diving at White Rock, we had a very funny incident. We were about 14 meters deep over sand, with coral-covered boulder outcroppings here and there. Lee, our instructor, was looking under a rock for

Our Koh Chang dive instructors

blue spotted stingrays. Not seeing any, he looked up, to see a pissed off titan triggerfish start to attack his fins as he swam away frantically. I barely noticed that my dad was also swimming away. I realize I'd better get out of there! I started to swim and the titan starts to come over, but instead of attacking me, it goes after my dad. Lee, being a hero, swam over and got the trigger's attention away from us. Eventually we got far away enough, so the trigger gave up, but I swear that trigger had a sixth sense. Before the dive, Lee said that he had never been attacked by a trigger, so he got attacked, my dad said he didn't want to be attacked, so he got slightly attacked, and me, I wanted to be attacked, but was passed by. Ironic, isn't it?

The divers' sign for it's all "OK", to say the least!

Koh Tao sunset

Sell Me A Beer?

I'm a minor, only 12 years old. In Santa Monica, my hometown, nobody, whether I know them or not, would let me near booze, but lo! Here in Thailand, while my parents were resting in a hot spring, I was walking up a dirt path to the refreshment stand violating that sacred rule. A few moments before, my parents had said, "Why don't you see if you can get us some beers?" They were joking, but I didn't know that at the time.

"Sure" I said. "Singha or Chang?"

"Chang."

"Okay."

I walked up to the stand about 1/2 a mile away and embarrassed said, "Can I have two Chang beers?"

"80 baht," the woman working there said. No questions, no strange look, no problem at all.

So fifteen minutes later, I returned with a couple of beers and a smile. My parents were dumbstruck, but pleased. You know, when you think about it, it's good thing I don't like alcohol!

Bliss is Gabriel Garcia Marquez in a hot spring river

Shawn's favorite spot in Pai

The Girl Next Door

Like all people, I have strengths, and unfortunately weaknesses as well. This story is about one of my weaknesses. Once I got up in front of my entire elementary school on "Disco Day" and danced with a student a year older than I. We were the only ones dancing in front of over 300 kids. I also ran for class president and won. I had no problem doing those things, which is one of my strengths. But I have the hardest time talking to anyone my age. I can only manage to say "Hi," and walk off. I may never see the kid again, but still, I just can't start a conversation. I wouldn't have any problem if the kid rejects me, and I'll be happy if he/she accepts me. But some nerve impulse won't let me talk. I just can't. Well, this is a story of that cursed impulse of mine that I wish would rot inside the deepest pits of hell.

We were in Pai for two weeks when it happened. It was near the end of our stay at the Golden Hut Bungalows. We had been there long enough to see neighbors move in and out. Two days before we left, I had come back early from an Internet café. When I walked up the stairs to our bungalow, I was on the balcony and right next to us, on their balcony was a very cute girl my age, reading The Lord of the Rings. As I was walking by, she looked up.

"Hi," I said.

"Hi," she replied.

I wanted to say something, say anything. I wanted to say, "Which Lord of the Rings book are you reading?" or "How long are you going to be here for?" or "hey, umm, well do you want to hang out?" or something like that, but instead I just smiled and walked into the bungalow never to see her again.

Our favorite, the Golden Hut Bungalows

One of many Stupas at the
King's Palace in Bangkok

A quick cross into Burma to renew our visas

Touring the Klongs (canals) of Bangkok

Starting on a 2 day white water raft trip
through the jungle of North Thailand
around Mae Hong Song

At sunset in Lod Cave thousands of swifts
enter the cave to roost just as thousands of
bats exit for the night

Firedancing show on Koh Phi Phi - I was inspired to take it up and do it now more than ever!

Every building erected must have a "spirit house" where the guardian spirits are given offerings daily

Northern Thailand on the road to Pai

In a Butterfly Garden in Koh Samui

Than Bokaranee National Park

Monkeys are really curious!

Lynda's Bad Day

How do you define a bad day? Something negative happens and immediately it's a bad day? I've had many "non-enjoyable days," but not many "bad" days. Poor Lynda had to have one on this trip.

To start off, she only got about 3 hours of sleep, on the day we were going to a waterfall. It was 20 kilometers away by motorbike. We organized the motorbikes like this: my dad drove my mom, Lynda's boyfriend, Dave, drove me, so that left Lynda to drive herself. Once we'd arrived at the waterfall she got stung by a bee, jumped up out of shock and soaked herself up to her waist. When we decided to leave the waterfall, and took off on the motorbikes, she panicked, and crashed. Of course she crashed into rocks, and it was a miracle that she came out with only a rather large bruise. She could no longer drive, so David took her back to our bungalows, but she was so relieved to be back that while getting off the bike she burned herself on the exhaust pipe!

Now that's a bad day! A disastrous day! A horrible day! What we love about Lynda though, is her sense of humor. Based on this day, she created the "Ass of the Day" awards! And I got a few awards myself!

Koh Chang Waterfall in the dry season

Lynda on a better day

Reggae Pub

Being only 12 years old, I never "hit" the club's before, but in Thailand, anything goes! My cousin T-C, my dad, my uncle, and I went to the Reggae Pub one night, and it was incredible. It was huge with 2 floors: a stage and a dance floor. There was even a live band playing. Well, I figured, what the heck, when they all got up to dance, I went along. Before I knew it, I was dancing with some Thai girls. Then I sat at our table and had a break; I did this all night; dance, take a break, dance, etc. Eventually, the band left to big applause and cheers, so a DJ started to play some music, but before that, he said "All right! Now were going to have a ... " His message became unclear, but we got the words "contest"…"win a beer and T-shirt"…"first guys then girls"…and "only 5 people." So T-C, figuring it's a dance contest tells me, "Yeah Josh go on up; it's a dance contest."

Being easy going, I said sure, so I hopped onto the stage, there were five people in the contest. It wasn't until they handed me a beer and interviewed me that I realized how much I was screwed. The host came up to me and said:

"What's your name?"

"Josh"

"Where are you from?"

"California"

And then he said to the audience, "All riiiight! this is Josh from the States."

Then he said:

"How old are you?"

"Twelve"

"Well, I'm not sure if it's legal, but hey, this is Thailand!"

Then he interviewed everyone else.

"Okay now," he said, "put the beer on top of your head, then on three, chug it, and when you're finished, place it up side down on your head!"

Well, I took a mouthful, and watched an Irish guy suck it down in 4 seconds flat! Even though I lost, my dad was happy; he got a free beer, and I got a great story to tell my friends!

The streets get busy at night

In the Ta Prohm Temple at Angkor Wat

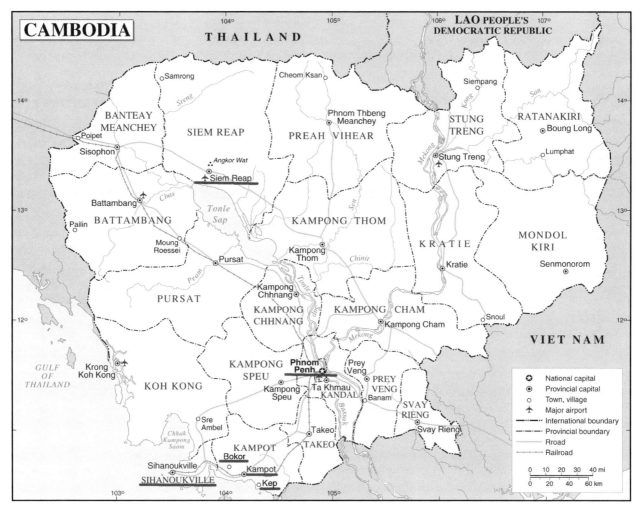

Places we visited underlined in red

Cambodia Information

Area: 181,035 square kilometers (about half the size of Germany)
Capital: Phnom Penh
Languages: Khmer, English, French, Chinese, and Mandarin
Money: US$1 =(approx) 3981 riel
Population: approximately 13.5 million
Religion: Theravada Buddhism, Hinduism

Government / Politics

Cambodia is a multiparty democracy under a constitutional monarchy since 1993.

Recent History

After the war in Vietnam, the Pol Pot regime took control of the government of Cambodia. Due to a belief that thousands of years ago, the Khmer people were excellent rice farmers, Pol Pot forced all of the people of Cambodia to go out into the rice fields and work all day, everyday. Anyone who resisted this regime, called the "Khmer Rouge" was executed. These were the "killing fields" of Cambodia - the most horrific thing ever to happen to this small country. In the rice fields massive holes were filled with human bodies. More than two million people were killed over the next three years from malnutrition, or assassination for stupid reasons such as they spoke a different language or they wore glasses. The Khmer Rouge were finally defeated in 1978, but the economy of Cambodia was destroyed, which resulted in a great famine where another couple hundred thousand died. By the end of all of this, there were few properly educated people left in Cambodia.

Historical Ruins

Angkor Wat is one of the most incredible places in the world, these legendary ruins are the most life changing places ever. The temples of Angkor are based off of the legendary Mount Meru in India, with five towers and moats (representing the Indian Sea) surrounding it. The most popular ruin in Angkor is Angkor Wat, considered to be one of the greatest architectural achievements in history, was built by the first god-king of Angkor. The moat surrounding Angkor Wat is over two football fields wide, the inner wall is more than two miles long and the central shrine is taller than Notre Dame cathedral in Europe. The towers of Angkor Wat imitate a closed lotus bud from the pools by its inner walls. When Angkor was at its peak in history it

Killing Fields Memorial in Siem Reap

The great Temple of Angkor Wat

had over a million people living there, while at that time London had only 30,000. The entire ancient city of Angkor is scattered over a site the size of Manhattan.

Temples you must visit at Angkor

Ta Prohm is a beautiful temple covered by the jungle, where <u>Tomb Raider</u> and other films were shot.

Bayon is a popular temple that has 216 gigantic faces of King Jayaavarman carved into stone on the 54 towers in the temple. It is very eerie, everywhere you look his face is staring back at you!

Bantei Srey is a temple about an hour's drive from Siem Riep that has incredibly intricate carvings in pink stone. It was one of the last of the temples found and one of the best preserved. It shouldn't be missed. All the ruins are worth seeing, but these are my favorites.

Other places that must be visited

Sihanoukville has one of the nicest beaches in Cambodia, and lots of good fresh food served to you right on the beach.

The fishing village near Sianoukville

45

Kep is a city on the beach in the south of Cambodia near Vietnam with a great history. Once it was a glamorous French town with huge colonial style houses that are now wrecked buildings taken over by jungle that you can climb through like a ruin. It was deserted during the time of Pol Pot.

Bokor is a hill station that was set up by the French to get away from the heat. Now it is a ghost town of ruined hotels and summer homes.

Abandoned Villa in Kep

Cambodia National Museum in Phnom Penh

At the King's Palace in Phnom Penh

Folks enjoying sunset on Sianoukville beach

Zorro

A stray wonders alone. Separated from the pack, it is sad and tired. That is how I felt until I met them. Back home there is always someone around, cousins, friends and sometimes adults. On this trip it's been just the opposite, only my parents and no people my age. When we were in Angkor Thom (a ruin of Angkor), my mom and I sat down to drink some water and catch a breather, when a boy walked by. My mom, being closer and quicker, says: "Hi, where are you from?"

"Oh hi, I'm from Australia. And you?" Before you know it, all three of us are in a lively conversation, when a woman arrived. "Oh there you are!" she says. Next thing you know, we all start another conversation. The boy's name is Zorro; his mom is Delfine. They live in Australia but his mom is French. Eventually, we decide it is time to leave, so we agree to meet at Ta Prom the next night.

Ta Prom, is a beautiful ruin covered in lush jungle. We arrived around 6 pm the next afternoon and didn't see our friends. As we walked inside I saw them sitting amongst the ruins, and boy was I happy! We explored Ta Prom that night by the full moon. For the next week we hung out with them at other sites, and did many things together. When we were in Phnom Penh, we stayed in the same hotel, and did some activities together. Later we went to Sihanoukville and Kep. It was so great to hang out with new friends. Zorro and I have much in common. We both love the Lord of the Rings series, almost all Sci-fi books, and many other things. Not being with people my age for a while was strange, but everything felt back to normal. A nice warm smile returned. We got to do a lot of things that most kids will never get a chance to do. I think we will be friends forever.

Zorro & Josh at Ta Sohm gate

Once, all the temples were overgrown by the jungle. While most have been cleared, a few such as Ta Prohm, have been left to show their condition when they were re-discovered in 1860.

Although now in ruins, the temples of Angkor actually have been in use since they were created

The walls of Angkor Wat are known for their immense bas-reliefs depicting ancient mythologies

*Celestial maidens called
"Apsaras" are carved
everywhere in Angkor*

*Kids everywhere loved to
come up and talk to us, as
here at Neak Pean*

*Monks can be tourists too,
such as these here at Bayon*

Bayone, the temple of hundreds of faces, built in the 12th Century by King Jayavarman VII

The main trees penetrating the ruins are the Kapok and the Strangler Fig

The gate of Ta Sohm

The face of Bayon is of King Jayavarman VII

Bantey Sri is one of the oldest temples in the region, and is made out of a pink sandstone. This small temple has some of the most intricate and delicate carvings in the country

The main temple of Ta Prohm was our favorite

Center of Siem Reap

Street market in Phnom Penh

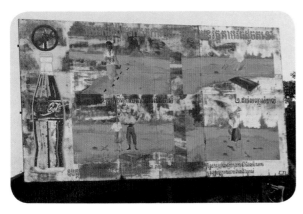

Billboard to explain landmine procedures

Visiting a silk factory

*Anything can ride on a bike,
note the pig is alive!*

*South of Siem Reap there is a Floating
village in Tonle Sap lake complete with
with floating gardens and animal pens*

Bayone Boys

Common sense. It is used constantly. It makes life easy and it never fails. Well, almost never fails, unless you don't follow it, and then fear can take over. Often I would hear stories of my parent's travels. Some were happy, while others were not. I would hear of possessions being stolen, people being robbed or threatened. When we were in the "Bayon" in Angkor Wat, I thought that the worst would happen to me. My parents and I split up, so we could look all around. While taking pictures, I noticed a small corridor, turning away from the main areas. Out of curiosity, I went along it to a small room, to take a couple of pictures, when I heard a voice, and spun around to face 3 boys who had followed me. They said the usual hello, where are you from, how old are you, so on and so forth. After a few questions, I smiled and walked out of the small room to a different set of bas-reliefs 50 meters away. While I was taking pictures, the same 3 boys came over and said that there were some nice sculptures 10 meters away. I followed them, but they weren't great, so I didn't take any pictures. But now, I was in a dark area away from people, and I let fear of the kids jumping me ensnare my mind, so I walked into a place farther away into the dark corridor. Of course I should have done

just the opposite - gone out into the crowds where I would have been safer. In the small, dark area, I stopped and realized I had done the wrong thing; I turned around to do the right thing, and saw the three boys in the doorway. I smiled and started to walk past, praying that they wouldn't attack me.

"Sir," said one of them "this sculpture very old, like 300 years."

"Akun (Cambodian for thank you)." I said and continued walking, a little faster now. "Oh sir," said the same one, who was following me.

"Yes?" I said.

"Could we have some money to go to school? Please sir, please." He said in a very childish voice.

Thinking that they would attack if I didn't give them money, I handed him 2000 Real, smiled, then continued walking.

"Eh-hem-hem," said the same boy, more forcefully, "2000 apiece please."

At this point I gave him two 2000 "Real" bills, then ran down the corridor to safety. I don't know if they would have caused me trouble or not, the thing that disappointed me is that my common sense knew better but I had not followed it. Hopefully we learn from these instances.

*On the upper levels
of the Bayon*

Landmine Experiences

War. It's what shapes much of the earth. Truly, it is. It's the beginning of the end. However, there is no complete end to a war because it leaves part of itself behind. Broken hearts, wounded people, parts of weapons or vehicles, ruined places, and worst of all, landmines.

Amoy lived on a farm with his family. Their oldest Cow, Sati, would sometimes wander away from their other livestock. One day, when Amoy was 9, Sati wandered very far away. Amoy was sent to bring her back. Sati was in an area Amoy had visited before. It was a common place where children would play. Amoy ran up the path to Sati, where she was grazing. Starting to walk her back to the herd, Amoy felt a red ant bite his ankle. He looked down and watched his foot come down on a land mine. He woke up inside a hospital, unable to feel his leg…it had been blown off and he was just lucky to be alive. There are thousands of stories you hear like this while you're in Cambodia. My mom had tried to warn me of all the amputees we would see, but nothing can prepare you…

Landmine warning signs are posted throughout much of rural Cambodia

Akira had been part of the Khmer rouge army, the Vietnamese army, and is now a de-miner. Not only that, but he owns a landmine museum that teaches people about landmine problems and he also houses and gives jobs to the kids who have lost their limbs. Mines in Cambodia have crippled 45,000 people and 120 more people are injured every month! It costs $5 to buy a mine, and $500 to remove one. They last up to a hundred years without disintegrating. In other words, it's the best soldier in the world. It never eats, never rests, and never misses.

Landmine Museum guide explaining the effects of mines

Bokor

Starting in the 1920's Bokor was a small hill station on the cliffs above Kep where the French and wealthy Cambodians would flee Phnom Penh to escape the summer heat. Then all hell broke loose during the Khmer Rouge era. All that is left is a ghost town of charred remains, stories, and spirits of the long departed. It was at least a six hour ride from Kep. Scratch that. It felt like a six-hour ride, but probably only lasted two hours. Once upon a time the road was paved. Now you'll be lucky it you get ten straight feet of

Peace on the Bokor Cliffs high above the coast

pavement. Anyways, you get the idea of a not-so-solid-very-bumpy-with-lots-of-rocks-in-the-road-in-the-middle-of-the-jungle-ride. Not so pretty, eh?

Our first stop was to be at the king's house. It was interesting, but nothing like what we were to see at the following places. Sorry, let me clear this up a bit. The king's place was awesome, really spectacular. It just seemed too, well too modern. The other buildings looked like old French architecture, the king's looked like a condo. As we continued, it seemed as if we were coming out of the jungle to a clearing. We came to the top of the hill and looked out to see grasslands. And then, looking closer, black outlines of buildings were visible scattered throughout the plains. A little bit down the hill, we lost sight of the buildings. We drove a little longer, not seeing anything but grass and the odd tree every now and then. Then before we knew it, we pulled up to a small monastery and we were greeted by smiling monks who were going to let us spend the night. As we started to unload our food, clothing, and other items, a monkey, who was one of the monk's pets, walked up and sat down, pulled up one of its legs next to his head, and then chattered his teeth. We had extra bananas, so we handed him a few. He gobbled then up, then walked away as we finished unloading. Once set up, we hopped back in the pickup truck (did I forget to mention that we were sitting in the back of a pickup the whole time we went up the crappy road?) and headed to the "Haunted Hotel".

Preparing for the ride up the hill to Bokor

After a ten minute ride we arrive at a large charred building. Zorro and I hopped out of the pickup and ran up to a man sitting in the doorway of the building and I asked: "What are the trucks here for?" "Make movies for Korea," the man replied. By now, my mom, dad and Zorro's mom had caught up, and we entered the building together. After an hour of exploring, getting lost, and finding each other, we learned that there were 5 levels, 4 terraces, and that this must have been a beautiful place at one time in history. We learned that it was once the "Bokor Palace Hotel". Later on we visited the beautiful one story Post Office. Then we sat on a high cliff that overlooked the jungle, and the ocean. The awesome thing is that we were at about the same level as the clouds; and the clouds next to the sun overlooking the valley, was a spectacular, absolutely incredible view.

After a little while we got back in the pickup and headed back to the monastery. We helped organize dinner, such as cutting and washing vegetables and carrying things back and forth. Once finished, Zorro and I had a stick fight in a little dried up pond. We didn't hit each other, but the monks sure got a kick out of it! Anytime we could we would play with the monkey. He turned out to be an adorable creature, who would play with our hair checking to make sure we didn't have fleas! It felt so good, like a massage. Finally it was dinnertime. We sat next to a pagoda and had the best meal we had in all

The Church once offered services to the French in the colonial era

The once-grand Bokor Palace Hotel and Casino

Inside the Hotel

The monkey loved to pick through your hair looking for lice and bugs, the most delicate massage you could imagine

of Cambodia. It was incredibly good Cambodian food, succulent lok-lak, great soup, tasty stir-fried vegetables in oyster sauce. After that satisfying meal our two guides made a fire from a plastic bottle, leaves, and twigs. We tried to explain to them that it punctured the ozone layer, but they wouldn't listen. By then we were really sleepy, so went to bed. I woke up late at night and looked over and saw the Buddha altar with a few candles burning in front of it with an orange glow, and a great comfort covered me.

We woke up early the next day, to catch part of the sunrise. I only saw the end of it, but it was majestic. After a breakfast of a baguette and fruit, we were ready to continue. We journeyed to the "Church." It was probably the spookiest place of all, even though it was daytime. The outside of the Church was covered in red moss, so it appeared to be stained with dried blood. The inside appeared unholy too. It seemed as if there was a sacrilegious worship table, to sacrifice people on. It wasn't very big, but was beautiful - for demons. Then we went to the haunted hotel again and we played a game of hide-and-seek in the hotel. I won because the objective of our warped version was to stay hidden as long as possible. I did the best tricks, like hide in the middle of a broken stairway, went through holes in walls, hid in places with multiple escape routes. Afterwards we went to a waterfall and climbed around there a bit, then got in the truck and headed back down the road from hell.

The Bokor Temple where we stayed the night

War. It's what shapes the earth. Truly, it is. It's the begginning of the end. ~~Breaking hearts, leaving wounded of this~~ However, there is no complete end to a war, because it leaves part of itself behind. Broken hearts, wounded people, parts of weapons, vehicles, ruined places, and worst of all, landmines.

Akira has been part of the khemer rouge army, the vietnamise army, and is now a de-miner. Not only all that, but he also owns a landmine museum, that teaches people about landmine problems. And a serious problem it truly is! 45,000 people are crippled by cambodia's mines, 20 more people every month. It costs 5US dollars, to buy a mine, and 500 to remove one. They stay up to a hundred years without breaking. In other words, the best soldier in the world. It never eats, never sleeps, never rests, and never misses.

This isare ae few storys of land-mines: (Please note, the names are fictional, stories are true)

Amoy worked, well, lived in a farm with his family. their oldest cow, Sati; would sometimes wander away from their other livestock. One day, when Amoy was 9, Sati had wandered very far away. Amoy was sent to bring her back. Now Sati was in a area Amoy had been before. It was a common place where children would play. Amoy ran up the path to Sati; where she was grazing. Starting to walk her back to the herd, Amoy felt a red ant bite his ankle. he looked down, and watched his foot come down on a land mine. He woke up inside a hospital, unable to feel his leg. And he still can't today.

Pha That Luang Royal Stupa in Vientiane

LAO PEOPLE'S DEMOCRATIC REPUBLIC

CHINA

CHINA

MYANMAR

VIET NAM

THAILAND

CAMBODIA

Gulf of Tonkin

- ⊕ National capital
- ⊙ Provincial capital
- ○ City, town
- ▬·▬·▬ National boundary
- ▬·▬· Provincial boundary
- ▬▬ Main road
- ▬▬ Secondary road
- ┼┼┼ Railroad
- ✈ Major airport

| 0 | 50 | 100 | 150 | 200 km |
| 0 | 25 | 50 | 75 | 100 mi |

Places we visited underlined in red

61

Laos Information

Area: 236,800 square kilometers
Capital: Vientiane
Languages: Lao and ethnic dialects
Money: US$1 = 7885 kip
Population: 5.8 million
Religion: Theravada Buddhism
The Name Laos means "Land of a Thousand Elephants" in the Lao language.
Government/Politics: The Laotian government is a Communist nation.

Places you must visit

Luang Prabang is a city that shows the culture of Laos better than anywhere else, and has the best night market. I highly recommend that you go there during the "Pi Mai Lao" festival, known also as Songkran. Throughout the entire city people stand in the streets with hoses and buckets of water and soak everyone who passes by. It is so much fun, an entire city water fight!

Vang Vien is a very laid-back town that is right next to a river with many caves carved into the limestone pinnacles. It is also a few kilometers from the mulberry farm, a place that you must visit. You can eat, work and sleep at the farm, any help you provide helps to keep the culture of local hill tribe people known.

Don Khon and Don Det are Islands all the way in the south of Laos bordering Cambodia on the Irrawaddy River. The Irrawaddy River is the home of the last of the freshwater Irrawaddy Dolphins, which you can watch playing and jumping at sunset.

Tat Kuang Si Waterfalls are 29 km south of Luang Prabang and are the most spectacular waterfalls I've ever seen! They have many levels for swimming and playing in the middle of pools in lush jungle!

Communist Victory Monument at the Kaysone Phomvihane Memorial in Vientiane

Pi Mai Lao

For New Years celebrations back home, we stay up late, party, and light off fireworks. Here in Laos, it is quite different. New Years comes in April and it is the hottest time of the year. The religious reason for the holiday is to clean the temple, Buddha images, your home, yourself, etc. With time it has turned into the biggest and best national water fight! They set up teams in the street and nail people with water, flour, grease and lipstick - all in good fun. People in cars, motorbikes, regular bikes and pedestrians are all prime targets. We were very excited to be here for this festival, it lasts a whole week and all the travelers had told us about it. We arrived in town a few days early to get set up. First we rented bikes with baskets and rode to the market to purchase buckets (that we put in the baskets), water guns, water balloons and cups for throwing water. The family we stayed with loved how ingenious our set up was! The first day till the last we would hit the streets, buckets full, armed and ready early in the morning until sunset, having nothing but fun.

Winners of the children's beauty contest

They have a big parade and even the monks carry umbrellas as they know they will be sprayed with water. This was followed by going to a holy island by boat where the local folks build stupas out of sand, then put drawings onto the stupa. They have a giant carnival, beauty contests and performances. At the National Luang Prabang Theatre, there was a performance of the Ramayana, it was a spectacular, with incredible costumes and live music. All in all, Pi Mai Lao beats our New Year celebration, every day was great and full of wonderful and wet events!

Celebrating Pi Mai Lao by soaking everyone you see

Monks in the Pi Mai Lao Parade

Boys who've been in the thick of it!

Getting ready for the evening watering

Our boys with Sam from the farm

"Ramayana" performance in Luan Prabang

At Pak Ou Cave

Pak Ou Caves

Average day. Had one basically every day back home. Here, no day is repetitive, ever. For our first day in Luang Prabong, I woke up late. The first thing I did was read, which to me is the best way to begin a day. Our parents decided that it was time for a bike ride, and before we knew it, we were off. We stopped at a beautiful restaurant overlooking the river and had breakfast, and an interesting breakfast it was! Al and I dueled over who ate the most green beans - it was pretty intense! Then we landed back at our hotel and after some discussion that I didn't hear between my mom and the hotel manager, arrangements were made to go on a boat trip along the Mekong River and then to go to the Nam Ou River to get to the Pak Ou caves.

With a short car ride and an even shorter walk, we were cruising down the Mekong River! After about 20 minutes of cruising the river forks and we take the left route. For the next 45 minutes, we were riding the Nam Ou River, seeing villages, people mining for gold, jungle, limestone pinnacles, and other incredible sights. At last we arrived at Tham Ting, the lower of the two Pak Ou caves. What a sight! Imagine this - a giant hole in a limestone pinnacle, great steps leading up to a wall of carved stone, appearing as if this had once been a fortress. Majestic, amazing, spectacular, beautiful! The basic sum of it is in those words. They are its invisible pillars, its greatest supporters. Once inside the cave, it only grew another pillar-wonderful! There must have been at least 500 Buddha statues. Most were quite small, but magnificent. It was the New Year so as part of their rituals they wash each and every Buddha, a very big job!

After that we went to the Tham Phun cave, which was slightly above the Tham Ting cave. The second cave was dark, which is always beautiful, especially because they light two candles next to a gigantic Buddha shrine - spectacular. There wasn't much else to see, so we left. Along the way back we stopped and watched some people panning for gold, which is a long, tedious process. We finished the afternoon by stopping in Ban Xian Hai, a village known for the huge amounts of jars they have. Then we had a sand ball war with my uncle Tiger. The Lao kids gave us some mean sand balls that crippled upon impact. It was a lot of fun playing and being crazy with a bunch of Lao kids.

Mekong Sunset in Luang Praban

Mulberry Farm

Just walking into the mulberry farm was nice; there were many plants, well-designed architecture and smiling people. A sign reading Phoudindaeng Organic Farm, comforted me. Organic, now there's a nice thing to boast about; not many farms, restaurants, or venders can. We sat down and ordered mulberry shakes and Zorro and I decided to split a mulberry pancake and Al ordered mulberry chips. After ordering, we took a dip in the Nam Song River because the mulberry farm was right next to it, pretty convenient. Eventually, our parents called us in to eat, and it was the best! The mulberry shakes were to die for and the pancakes were exceptional!

Boys & young mulberry plants

After eating God's food, we met Sam who was staying here and working at the organic farm. He was a nice guy with a lot of knowledge about the place. The owner, Mr. T, has operated this farm by himself with no funding other than donations. The farm takes up an area of six hectares and has 6000 mulberry plants. He told us that it was founded eight years ago to help develop as a co-op farm for the local hill-tribes to work together to produce silk. Now the farm is producing around 40 kilos of silk per year. People work with the catepillars, prune the mulberry plants, make silk thread and weave the thread into products. Sam took us on a short tour of the mulberry farm, and then we returned to the café. On the way back though, I noticed a poster that had "education" written on it, so I read it. It told about how students had to bike to and from school every day, which

Hanging out with the kids from the school

ended up in many accidents along the road. Recently, it read, we have received a school bus to pickup and drop off students every day, but we need your contributions to keep the bus running. A worthy donation, I must say. Then it was time to leave and I said to Sam "Maybe we'll see you again sometim..." Little did I know that we would be seeing him soon. The day after that visit, our parents left us to play for a while, but we didn't know where they went. Later that night (the day after the visit to the farm), our parents asked us this incredible question. "Would you boys like to stay at the organic farm, without us around, but you have to work and do all the different jobs?" "Yes!" We all screamed!

Bagging rice husks for later use in brick-making, nothing goes to waste!

We woke up early the next morning to go to the mulberry farm. Sam showed us our room, which was huge, beautiful, and overlooked part of the farm. We spent the next few days rising at sunrise to prune plants, shovel rice husks into bags, build the weir (dam); eating, sleeping, swimming, meeting other people, playing games, and for Al, inventing a new card game called "Islands." The part I'll miss the most though, is going to the community center at around 5:00 pm to teach the Kmou, Hmong, and Lao children English. I'll never forget the time Al and I taught them hopscotch. Memories forever. All of this was an experience I'll never forget. The only part I want to forget is how sore some of our joints were afterward!

This is the small "weir" we built to help divert the water away from the riverbank by the farm

Tat Kuang Si

We went to the Tat Kuang Si waterfall during the Pi Mai Lao water festival. It was a long tuk-tuk ride to get there, it must have lasted forty-five minutes. When we would pass through villages, the locals would throw water at us and we would get soaked! We loved it! Once there we walked up the path to get to the waterfall. On the way we stopped and saw a captive white tiger, he was beautiful and had a large jungle habitat to live in. We stayed to watch him eat some raw meat and he had the same movements as my cat Shammy - pure beauty.

We continued up the path and arrived at the waterfall. It was incredible, turquoise pools all around us. There were a couple of small waterfalls and one huge waterfall. We went to the big waterfall first, and swam behind it, which wasn't easy as it had a very strong current. Then we climbed up on the rocks, and jumped into the spray. It took some nerve to do it the first time, but then we couldn't stop. Awesome! Afterward we went down into some deeper pools, and after testing, we found a spot where we could jump in, that was a ton of fun. Later, we decided to take the path up to an area above the falls. After a long and sweaty climb to the top of the falls through the jungle, we realized that there were four levels! We climbed down to the third level, where quite a few people were, with a nice, large pool, and some other things that we couldn't see at the moment. At the third level, we jumped into the pool, and climbed all over the place until Al found a cave behind a small waterfall and I found a small catacomb of caveways. We needed a flash light and my uncle had one. I've always wanted to see a cave behind a waterfall. We disappeared for a long while, and when we came out there were a dozen monks in saffron robes at all different levels in the water. It was a beautiful sight, the orange on the monks, blue water and green jungle, what colors! We played at all levels for hours and didn't head home until sunset. What a great day! The best waterfalls I may ever see in my whole life! It was so great we went back several times before we left Luang Prabang.

Arriving at the waterfalls

It's easy to make friends here

Buddhist monks enjoying the waterfalls of Tat Kuang Si

☐ of the mulberry plants   ☐ of this

Later that night (the day after the visit to the farm),
our parents asked us this incredible question. They
asked: "Do you guys want to stay at the organic farm,
without us around, but, you have to work there, do
all the different jobs."
"Yes."   ~45

We woke up early the next morning, to
go to the mulberry farm. Sam showed us
our room, huge, beautiful, overlooking part of
the farm. Well, to sum it up easily,
we spent the next 2½ days pruning
(in which we cut off the small parts □ and the
parts which grew outward), shoveling rice
husk into bags, building the wer (dam), eating,
sleeping, meeting other people, playing games,
and for al, inventing a new card game
called "islands". X. All ☐ was an experience I'll
never forget. X. The only part I want to
forget is how sore some of our joints
were afterwards.   100

X the part I'll miss the most though, is going
around 5:00 pm to the community center and
teaching the Kmou, Hmong, and Lao kids english.
Like, I'll never forget the time al and
I taught them hopscotch. Memories forever.

What we did w/ rice husk, How our day went, How we
built the wer, playing in the river,

We woke up early to go to the mulberry
farm. Sam showed us our room, huge, beautiful,
overlooking part of the farm. Our first
day we started by pruning (which is when you
take clippers and cut off the small parts
of the mulberry plants and the parts growing
outwards), then we ate a meal and met
some of the other people staying here,
then we pruned some more, then we went
swiming in the river, then we ate, then
we relaxed/played games/met people, then
we worked on the wer (in which we build
a dam in the river to help divert
water, and force the current to go the other
way. We built the wer out of rocks, from
the river or the bank.), then went to
the community center to teach kids english, then
went back to the farm and ate, then slept.
The next day we pruned, then ate, then shoveled
rice husk into bags (to use in the making of
adobe bricks, or to put at the base of
mulberry plants to keep away weeds, or
other things), then relaxed, then ate, then worked
on the wer, then went to english teaching
class, then slept. for day three we pruned,
ate, relaxed, we red, then left the mulberry farm

71

Schwedagon Pagoda, Yangon

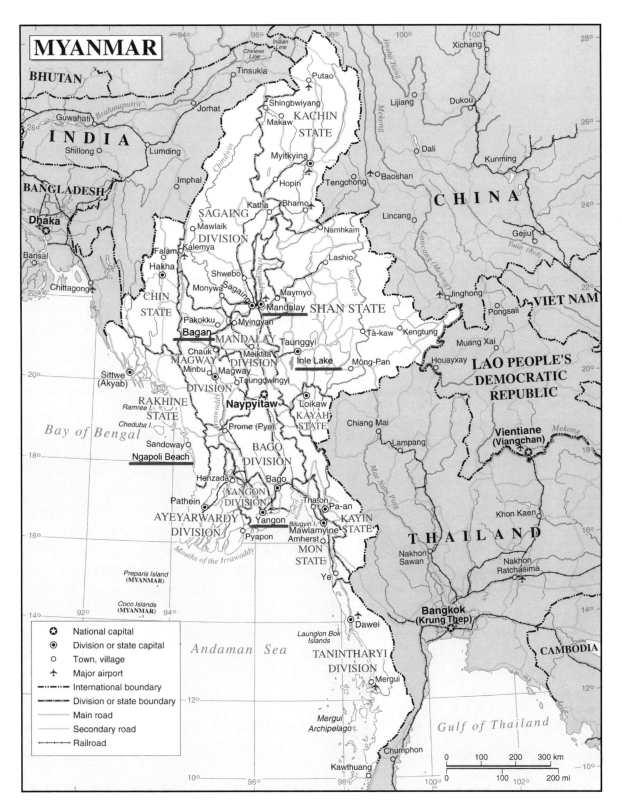

Places we visited underlined in red

Myanmar Information

Area: 671,000 square kilometers
Capital: Yangon
Languages: Burmese, English
Money: US$1 = 6.45 kyat = 1 FEC
Population: 49 million
Changed name from Burma in 1989
Religion: 87% is Theravada Buddhist, but Hinduism, Christianity and Nat worship are common too. Nats are spirits that inhabit natural features or humans, whether for good or evil. Nat worship was practiced before Buddhism, and once Buddhism became the larger religion, Nats were integrated into the stories and practiced alongside Buddhism.

Government / Politics

The government of Myanmar is an opressive totaliarian regime. While traveling in Myanmar we made every effort not to support the government. This was pretty easy, we never went to any government owned hotels, restaurants or other facilities as much as possible. This way we helped the people but not the corrupted government.

Aung San Suu Kyi is the daughter of one of the modern founders of this nation who was assasinated in 1947. She became the leader of the National League for Democracy then was attacked and put under house arrest by the government to stop her from speaking against the government. Even after her arrest, Aung San Suu Kyi continues to speak out to promote Democracy in Myanmar.

Places that you must go

Bagan is a town that has thousands of pagodas, shrines, and temples; it is an ancient city and is breathtaking.

Inle Lake is a beautiful body of water in Myanmar. There are temples and towns built on top of pushed-up mud. Most houses and temples are on stilts, and it is amazing the way you are surrounded by water in a holy temple. The only way to get there is by boat. There has been recent attention brought to a certain temple on the lake, commonly known as the "Jumping Cat Monastery" where the monks have trained cats to jump through hoops about 3 to 4 feet off the ground. There are floating markets, and it is a spectacular sight to see, all of it.

Ngapoli Beach is a beautiful coastal area that is just developing, and since there is almost no one there, it still has the flavor of Myanmar.

Yangon and Mandalay are the two largest cities which have some amazing temples and old architecture.

Most women and children beautify themselves with "Thankakha", a traditional yellow cosmetic held in great esteem

The ancient King's Palace in Mandalay

Happy kids on Inle Lake

Renovated Buddha in old ruins in Nyaungshwe

Novitiate monks learning in
the Schwe Yaunghwe Kyaung
Monastary near Inle

Ngapoli Beach is a
beautiful area targeted
for future development,
but it is still pretty wild

Inle Lake

Our adventures in Nuang Shwe on Inle Lake included a few boat trips. What is unique about this lake is that it is so shallow that boatmen have learned to propel and steer their boats standing up with one foot on the oar/tiller. That way they can look ahead and stay clear of trouble. One boat ride took us to the "Jumping Cat Monastery", where we met a really nice monk who showed us around and gave a small performance of cats jumping through hoops. Here they have trained cats to jump through hoops three feet off the ground on command. At this monastery there were over 50 cats, and the monastery was in the middle of the lake. Besides that, it was just a beautiful temple on the lake.

We went to a place where lotus stalks are woven. They take the filaments of a lotus stalk, allow them to dry, and twist them into thread then weave them into cloth. They use a special material to make the monks their robes. We visited many different temples including the most holy temple on the lake, the Phaundaw Oo. It was there that I had my first chance in six months to play the piano, and I was lousy. I couldn't remember anything. Another stop was to an umbrella making shop where they use mulberry wood bark to make paper umbrellas and then flowers are pasted on the top. All the markets we visited were interesting. There was a floating market

A young novitiate rides to his new monastary in a parade surrounded by family and friends

Boatmen on Inle Lake have developed a way of rowing with their legs

Nga Phe Chaung, "jumping cat" Monastary

designed for tourists and a market on land, which was for the locals, I liked that market much more.

When children turn ten years old they are expected to spend three months in a Monastery being a monk. It is a very special time. The parents are very proud and spend whatever they can on the celebration. We were lucky to be here at this time and go to a few of the festivals. In the first one, we went to a child's house and drank a little tea while watching the celebration while there was dancing and music. The second time, a parade came down the street with many people, comedians, musicians, and a horse that the novice monk rides, dressed as Young Siddhartha. At the third festival, we went to a Wat and saw the ceremony where a child was presented with his monks robes. I was amazed at how welcome we always felt at these places. It was hard to leave, we loved the people who we had lived with and had so much fun with.

A cat hits the hoop

Fishermen in the shallows of Inle Lake

A floating market now mostly sells to tourists

Herb seller at a regional market

Hell Ride to Bagan

Inle Lake was a nice, cool, relaxing place to be. But we couldn't stay there forever. The next spot that we visited on our journey through Myanmar was Bagan, a town next to a river that had tons of chedis, stupas and temples. At our hotel in Nuang Shwe, we had arranged for a van to take us to Bagan.

The next day started early, we hopped into a van at 6 a.m. with two nice drivers. We drove 3 of the 8 hours this trip was to take, and the car broke down. It wasn't working at all, and we were in the middle of nowhere. We left at six thirty and by now after 3 hours of waiting, it was 12:30. It was around 12:45 when we finally got it working. We traveled maybe 1000 feet and it broke down again, but we were close to a few small huts this time, so we went to them and talked to some local Burmese people. We waited for an hour, and then a truck came by, so we hitched a ride sitting on cement bags (pretty comfy) in the back.

When you break down in the middle of nowhere here, the driver will tear apart the engine and start repairs on the spot!

The van and the two Burmese guys who were driving it were left behind, they promised to catch up. The truck took us to a city, and dropped us off at a restaurant where our drivers told him to leave us. We sat there for a little while and before we knew it, it was 2:30.

Eventually we said, "Screw it" and we hopped a ride with a "songtaew", a pick-up with lots of people packed in. We got to ride up on the top of the truck on our way to Bagan! We were on the songtaew for a while when honk-honk! It was our drivers in the van, so the songtaew pulled over; we got back in the van and continued the journey. Well, we trudged on for a while with not many problems. Every once in a while we had

We were welcomed warmly by people close by who opened their homes to us while we waited

to stop in a town to let it cool down and give the van more water.

By now it was 5:00, and "just because we're so close," we headed to Mt. Popa, the holy mountaintop where all the "Nats"(ancestor gods) live - it was kind of spooky! Maybe it was the night (by now it was 6:30), maybe it was the fatigue, either way, I disliked Mt. Popa. Back in the van I passed out in 10 minutes and I can barely remember arriving at a hotel at 11:00 at night. We had been on the road since 6 am! A trip that should have taken 8 hours took 17 hours! My mom said from now on we fly in Myanmar!

I tried to communicate by using a dictionary, but much more was expressed non-verbally.

Our 2nd leg was in the back of a delivery truck

After the truck, we took a local "songtaew" for a while before our original van was fixed many hours later and actually found us on the road to take us the rest of the way!

79

Bike Riding in Bagan

"Mom, c'mon I don't want to."

"Josh, you're going whether you like it or not."

"It's too damn hot."

"Honestly Josh, it's really close, you're going, you'll love it."

Well, it was decided. We were going to a temple in Bagan by bicycle. As we passed outside the gate, everyone was already sweating. We looked down the road in both directions and there was no one, nothing, no cars or buses, the road was vast empty space. We took a right and started to pedal. We stopped after about 7 minutes of pedaling, and we all drank so much water, our supply was nearly gone. So we continued, pedaling slightly uphill. A lone motorbike came down the road, and a monk on the back looked at us and waved a finger and shook his head as if to say, "Are you guys crazy?" It was 44° C, which is about 112 degrees Fahrenheit. Little did we know that in Myanmar, Bagan means, "Parched earth." However, we did see some stupas with Buddhas inside of them as we rode by.

Thatbinyu Paya at dawn

Well, we nearly had heat strokes, but we got there! We stopped at a restaurant, drank lots of liquids, and took a boat home. There was no way in hell (and this was hell) that we were pedaling back. I'm happy to say we never did that again!

The next morning my parents woke me up at 4:30AM. Now, we were going to try early morning bike rides. No matter how much I pleaded, we were going to go. As we set out, it was still really dark, and we rode to the entrance of old Bagan before we broke a sweat. We rode pretty far into old Bagan, stopping at temples and stupas on the way. We even caught a great sunrise, so I guess the trip wasn't too bad even though I hated getting up early. Then we started the ride back and it was starting to get hot. We got back by nine o'clock and jumped in a pool! From then on we biked from 4AM to 9AM and from 6PM to 10PM, this way we didn't get deep-fried!

Josh at Mingalarzedi Pagoda, the last of the large late period temples, built in 1277

There is at least one statue of the Buddha in almost all of the Temples. This is one of four in the Ananda Temple

There are over 2000 pagodas and temples on the plain of Bagan, some more than 1500 years old

Schwezigon Pagoda is the center of current Buddhist practice in Bagan

Manuha Paya is another very active temlple

Htilominlo Temple was built in 1218

Dhammayangyi Temple is the largest one

Dhammayangyi's Twin Buddhas

Mt. Popa is a volcanic outcropping near Bagan which is the spiritual home of the "Nats" which were worshipped before Buddhism arrived

Figures of the Nats in the temple on the top of Mt. Popa. The Nats are often revered equally with the Buddha

Monks leaving Manhua Paya

Part of a celebration is the offering of alms and rice to the monks

Most of the areas in between the temples are planted with crops

The Best Restaurant in Yangon

When I was little, I would eat with my hands. Now that I'm older, I get a second chance. I wonder, is that a good thing? "Just take us to your favorite restaurant!" my mom told the taxi driver. I though she was off her rocker. I thought he was just going to choose a restaurant at random. But then, why was he making so much effort searching? At last, we arrived. As we walked in we saw the most peculiar of things! To start, some people were eating off banana leaves, and everyone was using their hands! We sat down and got a quick briefing, my mom, having spent months in India in her youth was very excited to fill us in.

"Alright now, this is an Indian restaurant, which means that you only eat with your right hand from the banana leaf. No matter what, only eat with your right hand! Under no circumstances are you allowed to eat with your left. You wash your hands before you eat, and well, that's it. You get rice,

Our "banana leaf" restaurant

Dried fish & chestnuts in a streetside market

A view down Maha Bandoola Street to the Sule Paya

different curries and Naan" (a special type of bread common to Indian meals). Later she explained that they wipe their butts with their left hand, that is why it's a strict rule - I don't blame them!

We waited a minute or so, and then the waiters brought us all metallic trays, but our parents quickly ordered banana leaves. In another minute, we all had banana leaves in front of us, then a guy came by and dumped a huge amount of steamed rice onto our leaves. Then comes another man behind him who puts four different small piles of curry onto the leaves. One of the curries is a red curry that was quite spicy; another is a yellow curry with chilies inside of it; the third is a yellow curry with mutton; and the last one is a spinach curry. Behind him is a man who brings out some dal (lentils) in a bowl. We feasted, because it was all you can eat - and it was the best food ever! We thanked our driver many times over as we ate and he knew we meant it as we went back every day from then on. I became very good at eating with my hands, my mom was worried I'd never go back to forks, and she should be! If I had my way.....

A woman selling owls and hawks on the street

Schwedagon Pagoda is the largest building in the world covered in gold. It is believed to enshrine four hairs of the Buddha given before he died.

Although mainly Buddhist, Hindu Temples can be found, such as this one in Yangon

Kuthodaw Paya houses the "World's Largest Book", each of the 729 little stupas has a marble tablet inscribed with a page from the Tipitaka canon of Theraveda Buddhism

A betel nut seller in Yangon

Waiting for a ferry across the Irawaddy River

Selling fish in a Yangon street market

Resting on a ferry in the Irawaddy Delta

Entrance to Twante Paya in the Delta region

Schwe In Bin Kyaung is a traditional Burmese monastary made of carved teak wood

Making & packaging gold leaf

Entrance to the stairway up Mandalay Hill which has a large temple on the top and many pagodas along the way

A traditional puppet show accompanied by musicians

The statue in the Mahamuni Temple in Mandalay is believed to have been created within Buddha's lifespan and so must have captured his true likeness. Devotees have covered the body with gold leaf, now 15 cm thick. Every morning at 4:30 AM monks wash his face and brush his teeth.

Inle lake. A nice, cool, relaxing place to be. But we couldn't stay there forever, 5 days infact. Our next spot on our journey through Myanmar was to be Bagan a place next to a river which had tons of chedis, stupas, and temples. At our hotel in Inle lake, we had arrangened for a van to come and take us to Bagan, so, the next day, we hop in the van to take us. So we drive 3 of the 8 hours, and the car breaks down. It wasn't working at all. We left at six-thirty and by now after 3 hours of waiting, it's already 19:30. It was around 12:30 when we finhaly got it working. So we travel, maybe 500 feet, and it breaks down again, and we wait half an hour, and then a truck comes by so we hop on the truck. So the van and the two burmese guys who were driving it are left behind. So the truck takes us to a city, and drops us off at a restaurant that our drivers told him to drop us off at. So we sit there for a little while, and before you know it, it's 2:30. Adventually we say "screw it" and hop a ride with a songtao heading to Bagan. And were on the songtao for a while when honk-honk. It's our drivers in the van, so we pull over, get back in the van, and continue the journey. Well we trudge on for a while with no problems. By now it's 5:00, and "just because we're so close", we head to mt. Popa. Maybe it was the night(by now it was 6:30), maybe it was the fatigue, Either way, I disliked mt. Popa. So then we had our last 3-hour strech to Pagan, in about 10 minutes I had passed out..... and I can barely remember arriving at our hotel, at 11:00 at night.......

Transport

How have we traveled back home? By car, bus, bike, plane, and walking. Here in Asia, it's incredibly different. We have all those and many more. There are long tail boats, which are 6 feet wide, and probably 60 feet long. We traveled on small motorboats and big ferry's; we did a lot of traveling by boats. Anytime we had a choice to get to our destination by boat or bus we always took the boat!

There are "tuk-tuks", which are 3-wheeled vehicles, with a passenger area and a driver's seat. Tuk-tuks are small vehicles that will take you anywhere in the city for a small price. There are "songtaews", which are basically a pickup truck with seats and a shade in the back. The songtaews can take you anywhere in the city or for longer distances if you like .

We've been on an ox cart and in a horse drawn cart, which is similar to the ox cart, except it was padded and shaded. We've been on motorbikes and in the sidecars of motorcycles. We've been in minibuses, its pretty much a van, except it's more cramped; they're also known as sardines in a can. To tell the truth, we've even been on the backs of elephants. We've been in a large bus that took us long distances, please note: this is very much unlike the bus transit system back home. There are jumbo tuk-tuks also know as mini songtaews that are much rarer.   Once we went on a thirteen hour sleeping train ride and because of various reasons (such as climate, closed windows, etc.), it was at least 41° Celsius in the train. It was a sweat storm!   I was lying naked in my compartment it was so hot! In a sauna you sweat less than you would in the train.   We have also been on bicycles many times, it was our favorite mode of transportation, and sometimes we would be in carts behind a motorcycle that someone else drove.   Where else in the world can you get such a great variety!

My first motorcycle ride,
3 on bike in Krabi, Thailand

Sunset on a commuter ferry on the Chao
Phrya River in Bangkok

Reflections

One year in Southeast Asia - the experience of a lifetime in my opinion. The wonders I have seen, the experiences I've had, the cultures I've witnessed, mystical they were, from the Angkor ruins, to the teak forests, to the different creatures, I've seen it all! But since the beginning of the trip, I knew it must come to an end. Days, hours, minutes before I left, it still had not sunk in, how could it? How could I come unto this realization? Traveling had become my life. The food was different. The religion was different. People's lives seemed opposite in America from Southeast Asia. It would be as weird to go back to America as it was to leave it. What would my friends be like? How would my city have changed?

In the last 20 minutes of the flight to LAX (LA Airport) I was just as anxious as I had been about 11 months ago, ready to explore a strange new land. Once we landed it took a good 45 minutes to get through customs and collect our bags. But once I had, I took the brave step out of terminal 2…

Epilogue

It is now a year later. I couldn't finish my book until school got out; and I'm kind of glad I didn't. As it has given me time to reflect, had I written this right away I would have felt very different.

When I started the eighth grade a year ago, school was pretty difficult. Studying in Asia was very different than normal school here. My friends had changed a lot, I barely recognized them, not just their faces, but who they were as a person. I had thought for a little while that the trip might have been a mistake. It might not have been worth it, for all the problems I was facing. After a few months into the school year, the problems started to work themselves out. I started to make new friends. I began to love the things that I had seen, the places that I had been, and of how it had changed who I am, I started to feel that the trip was worth it no matter what! Often I have memories of our trip, and how much I miss it now, and I thank my parents for this magical journey.

One effect of this trip was to get me hooked on traveling, I can't wait until I'm older and can hit the road again! I have to say, above all else, this trip has taught me things that nothing else could have. It has taught me how to soar above the orchids and not get caught beneath the ferns.

September

October

November

December

January

February

May

June

July

93

Joshie's Hungry! - Assorted Asian Dishes

Som Tam or Green Papaya Salad
Rating: 5/5 (when you get a good one)
Ingredients: sliced, thin, long strips of green papaya, salt, sugar, dried shrimp or crabs (optional), peanuts, chili's and sometimes other items, every chef makes their own unique (not recommended for people who don't like it hot).

Pad Thai or Thai noodles
Rating: 3-4/5
Ingredients: rice, glass or Thai noodles, various vegetables, various spices, ketchup (make sure they don't add too much), Pad Thai is stir-fried in a wok (large frying pan).

Massaman Curry
Rating: 4/5
Ingredients: yellow curry with coconut milk, potato chunks, meat or tofu.
Description: Yellow curry with no vegetables besides potato chunks, unless otherwise desired, more common in the north.

Green Curry
Rating: 3.5/5
Ingredients: a sweeter green curry with coconut milk, meat or tofu, vegetables.
Description: green curry with meat or tofu and vegetables, more common in south.

Red Curry
Rating: 3/5
Ingredients: a spicier red curry with coconut milk, meat or tofu, vegetables.
Description: red curry with meat or tofu and vegetables.

Pnaeng Curry
Rating: 2/5
Ingredients: red or yellow curry with lots of extra dry spices, meat or tofu and vegetables. Usually comes with herbs inside.
Description: Pnaeng curry with meat or tofu and vegetables.

Fish balls
Rating: 2/5
Ingredients: Small gray balls made out of fish and ?

Kao Soy
Rating: 4.5/5
Ingredients: yellow curry with potato chunks, safari mushrooms, crispy wontons, rice or glass noodles, tofu.
Description: a Northern dish.

Sate
Rating: 3.5/5
Ingredients: meat on a stick, sometimes comes with sweet cucumber salad and peanut sauce.v
Description: grilled meat.

Fresh Spring Roll
Rating: 1/5
Ingredients: rice paper for wrap, fresh lettuce, sometimes it has mini-shrimp.

Fried Spring Roll
Rating: 3/5
Ingredients: fried outer rice, fried cabbage, similar to an egg roll.

Various Gelatin Cubes
Rating: 2.5/5
Ingredients: gelatin, coconut milk, contains various artificial flavorings, common in Laos.

Thai Pancake
Rating: 4/5
Description: a dessert a small amount of dough flattened out, fried on a large hot plate, can come w/ the following: egg, banana, chocolate, condensed milk.

Shrimp crackers
Rating: 4/5
Description: They taste similar to pork-rinds with out the meaty taste. Usually served w/ a sweet and sour sauce.

Shan noodles
Rating: 3/5
Description: Really, really "stick-to-your-ribs" greasy. Rice noodles served in gravy with few vegetables. Fattening but delicious.

Hill Tribes

Karen

Population: 322,000
Origin: Myanmar
Present Locations: Thailand, Myanmar
Economy: rice, vegetables, livestock
Beliefs: Animism, Buddhism, or Christianity
Characteristics: The Karen Women are known for their unique elongated necks, which are produced by silver bracelets worn around their necks, once they have done this they can never remove them or their necks will break. They do this for beauty. The Karen hill tribes wear thickly woven V-tunics of multiple colors. The Karen Tribe use crop rotation rather than the more common slash and burn technique. The Karen are divided into four different groups: the White Karen (Skaw Karen), Pwo Karen, Black Karen (Pa-o) and the Kayah Karen. Together, the Karen groups make up about half of all hill tribe people.

Akha

Population: 48,500
Origin: Tibet
Present locations: Thailand, Laos, China, Myanmar
Economy: rice, corn, opium
Beliefs: Animism with an emphasis on ancestor worship
Characteristics: The Akha wear headdresses of beads, feathers, and dangling silver ornaments.

Hmong

Population: 124,000
Origin: southern China
Present locations: southern China, Thailand, Laos and Vietnam
Economy: rice, corn, opium
Beliefs: Animism
Characteristics: Hmong tribe people wear black jackets, indigo shorts or skirts, and silver jewelry. Most of the Hmong people live near the city of Chiang Mai

Lahu

Population: 73,000
Origin: Tibet
Present locations: southern China, Thailand and Myanmar
Economy: rice, corn, opium
Beliefs: Theistic Animism, Christianity
Characteristics: The Lahu people wear black and red jackets with narrow skirts for women. The four groups of Lahu people consist of the Red Lahu, the Black Lahu, the Yellow Lahu and the Lahu Sheleh.

Lisu

Population: 28,000
Origin: Tibet
Present locations: Thailand, China
Economy: rice, corn, opium, livestock
Beliefs: Animism with ancestor worship and spirit possession
Characteristics: The women wear long multicolored tunics over trousers and are known to sometimes wear black turbans with tassels. Men wear baggy green or blue pants that are pegged at the ankles. They often wear many bright colors.

Mien

Population: 40,000
Origin: central China
Present locations: Thailand, southern China, Laos, Myanmar and Vietnam
Economy: rice, corn, opium
Beliefs: Animism with ancestor worship and Taoism
Characteristics: Women wear black jackets and trousers decorated with embroidered patches and red fur like collars along with dark blue or black turbans. The Mien culture has mainly been influenced by the Chinese, they use Chinese symbols to write their language, and they still carry out many Chinese traditions.

Hotels - Thailand

Bangkok - New Siam 2

It is a more modern hotel that is close to Khaosan road. The guesthouse has a swimming pool, computer café, and restaurant. Not overly priced, around 200-400 baht per night, depending on number of people. Close to the river.

Koh-Samui - Chaweng Gardens

A guesthouse with a selection of rooms with air conditioning, T.V., and higher quality bathrooms/room in general for around 800 baht per night; or bungalows with a fan and lower quality room for around 250-400 baht per night depending on whether you want two-four people stay in the room. It is about a thirty-second walk to the beach from your room. The restaurant at Chaweng gardens is the best for sitting on the beach and having a cool drink.

Koh Phangan - Mae Had View Bungalows

A great place to live, this tiny secluded beach has many bungalows directly on the beach that are very cheap.

Koh Phi-Phi - Chao Koh Resort

It is a good place to stay, despite the fact that it is more expensive-1000 baht per night, around 25 US dollars. However, I am not completely sure if it is still there, after the tidal wave hit.

Koh Lanta - Lanta Nice Beach

A beautiful, very cheap bungalow resort, that is of great quality, 500 baht per night for luxury. It is run by a kind Muslim family that if you are there for Ramadan, they will celebrate it with you, really lovely people.

Krabi - Grand Tower Hotel

Great place to stay – close to where you catch the boats for the islands

Chiang Mai - Top North Guest House

It is a guesthouse with a big selection of rooms and good food at the restaurant there. It is close to the night-market and the Sunday market. Has a pool and rooms cost anywhere between 200-1000 baht per night.

Pai - Golden Hut Bungalows

Probably one of my favorite places that we stayed the entire trip: beautiful bungalows overlooking a small river with rice paddies and jungle on one side and a temple on the other, really incredible. The bungalows are very well priced too.

Koh Chang - White Sands Resort

It is a remote bungalow resort that you get to by walking for 20 minutes down the beach or must take a boat to. It is a place that has little electricity-it goes out around nine. Though these two things, it is very well priced and makes you feel like you are on your own little island, you are right on the water that is crystal clear.

Koh Tao - Coral Grand Resort

This island and resort is really only for people who dive. The rooms here cost a lot of money unless you have signed up for a course or more than 10 dives, in which case they allow you to stay in one of their smaller, "economy" rooms that are still good, but nasty compared to the expensive ones.

Hotels - Cambodia

Siam Riep - Reaksmey Chanreas

This guesthouse is found in the middle of the city of Siam Riep, it has large rooms and is a little high priced.

Phnom Penh - Bright Lotus 1

A decent little guesthouse, however there are many flights of steps up and down that get quite tiring after a while. Get a room with a balcony, you look out upon the National Museum. One block to the river.

Sianoukville - Apsara Guesthouse

This guesthouse is not of the best quality but is decent, nice people run it.

Kep - Veranda guesthouse

Most likely one of my other favorite guesthouses ever, this one is built on a hillside over looking the ocean and the walkways between bungalows are suspended over bamboo. At the restaurant, the food is of excellent quality and the people are the nicest ever, it probably is one of the best guesthouses ever.

Hotels - Laos

Vientienne - Saysouly guesthouse

A guesthouse that is in the center of town and is of decent quality for its location.

Vang Vien - Riverside Bungalow

These bungalows are incredible, though not the most luxurious, are beautiful. You are right on the river, you have an open grass field in front of you and you are out of the center of town. However, another incredible place to stay at is the Mulberry farm a few miles away.

Champasak - Saythong guesthouse

A guesthouse that is relatively small and very cheap- both in price and quality. You are right on the river though.

Luang Prabang - Tanoy Guesthouse

It is a great guesthouse for large groups like we were. It is owned by a lovely Lao family who invited us to celebrate Pi Mai Lao with them. Very cheap rooms, overall a great place to stay

Hotels - Myanmar

Mandalay - Royal Gardens guesthouse

A very cramped guesthouse that was one of our lower quality guesthouses we stayed at.

Inle Lake(Nwang Shwe) - Aquarius Guesthouse

A very good Guesthouse with good rooms for their price, you're very close to the river, very friendly people own it, and the people who own it can arrange tours or transportation for you.

Bagan - Golden Express hotel

This hotel is a more expensive one and it supports Myanmar's oppressive government, the only reason that we stayed there is because Bagan is so hot, you can't go out into the city from around 8 a.m. to 6 p.m. and it was the only hotel with air-conditioning and a pool. And trust me, without those two things Bagan would have been hell.

Ngapali - Linn Thar Oo guesthouse

This guesthouse was very nice, it was beautiful and you had your window overlooking the beach, it was a great place.

Basic Thai Glossary

Sawatdee	- Hello		

Sawatdee - Hello
Kap kun ka/krap - Thank you
Yes - Ka/Krap
No - Mai
Pom - Me
Kun - You
Utinae* - Where is….
Hong nam - Bathroom
Rong ram - Hotel
Ran-ahan - Restaurant
Ta lat - Market
Su nam bin - Bank
Mapaoo - Coconut
Malako - Papaya
Ruiga - Boat
Muay Thai - Thai boxing
Rot - Car
Rot mei - Bus
Rot fai - Train
Rot chachaiyan - Bicycle
Tahu - Tofu
Kgai - Chicken
Tiang - Bed
ppajom - Blanket
ppaputinon - Sheet
pillowmon - Pillow
Bogmon - Pillow case
Koweee - Chair
Gaonam - Drinking glass
Nam - Water
Pet mai - Is it spicy
Choke dee - Good luck
Lot noy dai mai - Lower the price
Dai mai - No way
Nam Nung** Kuat - One water please
Put Thai dai mai - Do you speak Thai?
Pak-pak Tahu (north)*** - Vegetables and tofu
Jayed tahu (south)*** - Vegetables and Tofu
Kun poot par sar angrit daimai
   - Do you speak English?

Numbers

Nung - One
Soung - Two
Sam - Three
See - Four
Haa - Five
Hok - Six
Jead - Seven
Pead - Eight
Kaow - Nine
Sib - Ten
Sib Ed - Eleven
Soung Sib - Twelve
Sam Sib - Thirteen
See Sib - Fourteen
Haa Sib - Fifteen
Hok Sib - Sixteen
Jead Sib - Seventeen
Pead Sib - Eighteen
Kaow Sib - Nineteen
Esseeb - Twenty
Esseeb Ed - Twenty-one
Esseeb Soung - Twenty-two
Esseeb Sam - Twenty three
Esseeb See - Twenty four
Esseeb Haa - Twenty five
Esseeb Hok - Twenty six
Esseeb Jead - Twenty seven
Esseeb Pead - Twenty eight
Esseeb Kaow - Twenty nine
Sam Sib - Thirty
See Sib - Forty
Haa Sib - Fifty
Hok Sib - Sixty
Hok Sib Soung - Sixty-two
Jead Sib - Seventy
Pead Sib - Eighty
Kaow Sib - Ninety
Nung Roi - One hundred
Soung Roi - Two Hundred
Sam Roi - Three Hundred
Nung Pan - One Thousand
Kaow Pan - Nine thousand
Nung Mun - Ten Thousand
Haa Mun - Fifty Thousand
Hok Mun Kaow Roi See Sib
   - Sixty Thousand, Nine hundred and Forty

*Utinae is used after a location, for example: Hong nam utinae(Where is the bathroom), or Ta lat utinae (Where is the Market).

** This phrase could also be used in a plural sense: Nam Ha Kuat(for five bottles)

*** When in the North or South, the Words may be different, or pronunciation may be different.

98

Made in the USA
Charleston, SC
09 December 2009